COVENTRY LIBRARIES

**Please return this book on or before
the last date stamped below.**

PS130553 Disk 4

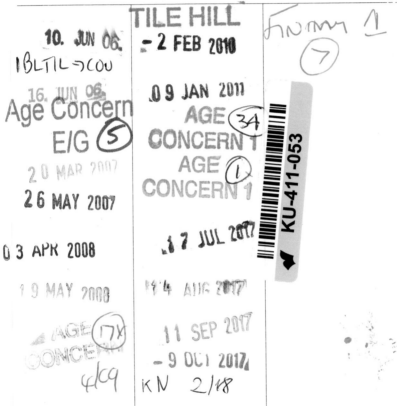
To renew this book take it to any of
the City Libraries before
the date due for return

SILENT NIGHT
THE REMARKABLE CHRISTMAS TRUCE OF 1914

Silent Night brings to life one of the most unlikely and touching events in the annals of war. The First World War had been underway for only a few months but had already been stalemated into the brutality of trench warfare. As Christmas approached, men on both sides—Germans, British, Belgians and French—laid down their arms and joined together in a spontaneous celebration with their enemy. For a brief, blissful time a world war stopped. Soldiers lit candles, decorated Christmas trees and serenaded each other with carols. Along the Western Front, troops from both sides ventured out into No Man's Land to exchange gifts, smoke, drink and even play football. Stanley Weintraub brilliantly conveys this strange episode, in this beautiful and moving account based on letters, diaries and firsthand records from both the German and the allied side.

SILENT NIGHT

THE REMARKABLE CHRISTMAS TRUCE OF 1914

Stanley Weintraub

CHIVERS PRESS
BATH

First published 2001
by
Simon & Schuster
This Large Print edition published by
Chivers Press
by arrangement with
Simon & Schuster UK Ltd
2003

940.4144

ISBN 0 7540 1856 3

British Library Cataloguing in Publication Data available

CONTENTS

Peace is harder to make than war.

A Stillness Heard Round the World:
The End of the Great War
(Stanley Weintraub, 1985)

For
Robert C. Doyle
and
Beate Engel-Doyle

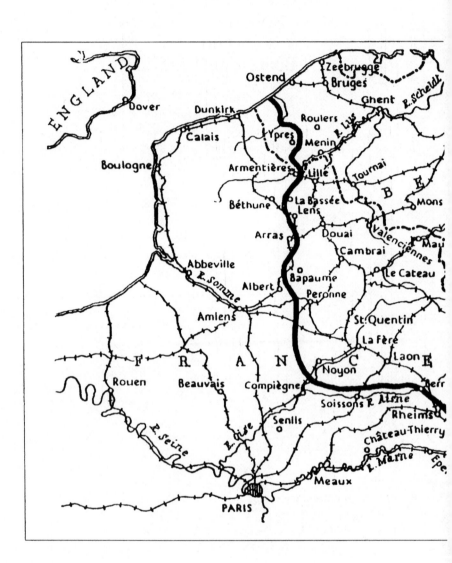

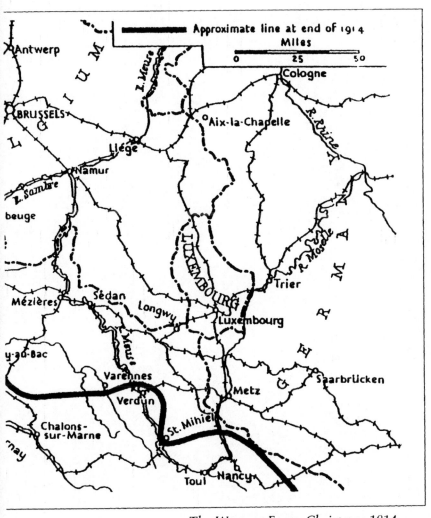

The Western Front, Christmas 1914.

SILENT NIGHT

SILENT NIGHT
THE REMARKABLE
CHRISTMAS TRUCE OF 1914

Stanley Weintraub

INTRODUCTION

Three myths would arise during the early months of the Great War. Burly Cossacks, sent by the Czar to bolster the Western Front, were seen embarking from British railway stations for Dover, still shaking the persistent snows of Russia from their boots. In France, during the British retreat from Mons, angels appeared—spirit bowmen out of the English past—to cover the withdrawal. And that, to the dismay of the generals, along the front lines late in December 1914, opponents in the West laid down their arms and celebrated Christmas together in a spontaneous gesture of peace on earth and good will toward men. Only one of the myths—the last—was true.

In an issue sent to press just before Christmas, *The New Republic,* an American weekly writing from a plague-on-both-sides neutrality, accepted what seemed obvious. 'If men must hate, it is perhaps just as well that they make no Christmas truce.' A futile resolution had been introduced in the Senate in Washington, urging that the belligerents hold a twenty-day truce at Christmas 'with the hope that the cessation of hostilities at the said time may stimulate reflection upon the part of the nations [at war] as to the meaning and spirit of Christmas time'.

Since early August the European war had claimed hundreds of thousands of killed, wounded, and missing. An appeal for a cease-fire at Christmas from Pope Benedict XV, elected just three months earlier, only weeks after war had broken out, had made headlines but was quickly rebuffed by both sides as 'impossible'. Rather, *The New Republic* suggested sardonically, 'The stench of battle should rise above the churches where they preach good-will to men. A few carols, a little incense and some tinsel will heal no wounds.' A wartime Christmas would be a festival 'so empty that it jeers at us'.

To many, the end of the war and the failure of the peace would validate the Christmas cease-fire as the only meaningful episode in the apocalypse. It belied the bellicose slogans and suggested that the men fighting and often dying were, as usual, proxies for governments and issues that had little to do with their everyday lives. A candle lit in the darkness of Flanders, the truce flickered briefly and survives only in memoirs, letters, song, drama and story.

'Live-and-let-live' accommodations occur in all wars. Chronicles at least since Troy record cessations in fighting to bury the dead, to pray to the gods, to negotiate a peace, to assuage war weariness, to offer signs of amity to enemies so long opposite in a static war as to encourage mutual respect. None had ever occurred on the scale of, or with the duration, or with the potential for changing things, as when the shooting suddenly stopped on Christmas Eve, 1914. The difference in 1914 was its potential to become more than a temporary respite. The event appears in retrospect somehow unreal, incredible in its intensity and extent, seemingly impossible to have happened without consequences for the outcome of the war. Like a dream, when it was over, men wondered at it, then went on with the grim business at hand. Under the rigid discipline of wartime command authority, that business was killing.

Dismissed in official histories as an aberration of no consequence, that remarkable moment happened. For the rival governments, for which war was politics conducted by persuasive force, it was imperative to make even temporary peace unappealing and unworkable, only an impulsive interval in a necessarily hostile and competitive world. The impromptu truce seemed dangerously akin to the populist politics of the streets, the spontaneous movements that topple tyrants and autocrats. For that reason alone, high commands could not permit it to gain any momentum to expand in time and in space, or to capture broad appeal back home. That it did not was more accident than design.

After a silent night and day—in many sectors much more than that—the war went on. The peace seemed nearly forgotten. Yet memories of Christmas 1914 persist, and underlying them the compelling realities and the intriguing might-have-beens. What if ...?

Late in December 1999 a group of nine quirky 'Khaki Chums' crossed the English Channel to Flanders with the 'blatantly daft idea' of commemorating the truce where it may have begun, near Ploegsteert Wood in Belgium. Wearing makeshift uniforms recalling 1914, and working in the rain and snow, they dug trenches, reinforcing them with sandbags and planks which 'literally disappeared into the bottomless mud'. For several days they cooked their rations, reinforced their parapets, and slept soaked through to the skin. They also endured curious onlookers and enjoyed visits from the media. Before departing, the nine planted a large timber cross in the quagmire as a temporary mark of respect for the wartime dead, filled back their trenches and slogged homeward.

Months later they were astonished to learn that local villagers had treated their crude memorial with a wood preservative and set it in a concrete base. In season, now, poppies flower beneath it. Thousands of Great War monuments, some moving and others mawkish, remain in town squares and military cemeteries across Europe. The afterthought of the Khaki Chums' lark in the Flanders mud is the only memorial to the Christmas Truce of 1914.

CHAPTER ONE

AN OUTBREAK OF PEACE

In December 1914, on both sides of the front lines in Flanders, astride the borders of Belgium and France, soldiers of two of Queen Victoria's grandsons, Kaiser Wilhelm II and George V, faced off from rows of trenches that augured a long war of attrition. Belgian and French forces were also along the line, and with the British and French were troops from India and Africa who had never seen winter snows. Opposite were not only Prussians, but Saxons and Bavarians and Westphalians who would rather have been home for the holidays. Christmas was approaching, a festive time common to all the combatants, from Russia in the East to England and France in the West. Some of its most resonant symbols were claimed by Germany, especially the Christmas tree, the *Tannenbaum* of carols sung in both languages. Gift-giving, the Yule log, even Santa Claus— St Nikolaus's name mispronounced—were also attributed to German custom, but long appropriated by both sides.

One of the few things about which the combatants agreed was the centrality of Christmas, but both sides also expected no let-down in the war. Separated by the miserable waste of No Man's Land as Christmas approached, troops seemed likely to enjoy nothing of the holiday's ambience—not even mere physical warmth. Cold rain had muddied and even flooded many trenches, and decomposing bodies floated to the surface. Crude 'duckboard' platforms barely kept soldiers dry, but few were eager to shelter in mucky hideaways that might be worse. Unless soldiers moved about, they would sink into the liquefying mud, and many slept erect if they could, leaning against the dripping trench walls. It was a stomach-churning atmosphere for eating one's rations. Latrines were nearly nonexistent and accomplishing bodily functions a nightmare. German Expressionist artist Otto Dix described the landscape of fortified ditches as 'lice, rats, barbed wire, fleas, shells, bombs, underground caves, corpses, blood, liquor, mice, cats, artillery, filth, bullets, mortars, fire, steel: that's what war is. It is the work of the devil.'

A lieutenant in the 143rd Lower Alsatian Regiment described German dugouts as desperate defences against nature. Candle stubs lit the dripping, rotting sandbagged walls. Floors were foul-smelling, 'viscous mush'. Sand-filled sacks hung from the ceilings not always successfully kept food from the reach of rats. Men deloused themselves by sizzling lice in the flame of a candle while others not so fortunate blew on their hands, seized rifles, and ascended for sentry duty. Relieved soldiers would stagger in, blinded by the candles, unbuckle and search for food. Then came sleeping. 'Eating and sleeping, standing guard, and, in between, trench digging,' one recalled, 'that was the routine.'

Much of the Ypres area was below sea level—a thin crust of soil concealing reclaimed swampland, dependent upon a disrupted drainage system. Yet as miserable as the mud was, the word was evaded, and mud slides were described as 'land-slips'. Trenches became—and echoed—home. The Durhams lay what they labelled the Old Kent Road, the Farm Road and New Road with bricks from 'ruined houses'. A strong point near Hoogstade was christened Clapham Junction; others were Battersea Farm, White Horse Cellars and Beggar's Rest.

Some German trenches were no longer awash, although rain and saturated meadows kept them soggy. Already dug in on slightly higher ground was an earthwork barrier, protected by masses of barbed wire, that left no flanks to turn and suggested that they might remain there until the other side wearied of the attrition. Both sides were unhappily expecting a long war. (It would be so long and bloody as to last only six weeks short of a fifth Christmas.) From the Channel to the Swiss frontier, neither side was yielding land in

7

which it was entrenched. The Germans were bringing in electric power and telephone lines, flooring deep-dug walkways, and constructing concrete machine-gun posts behind the first rows of trenches. But concerned that troops might not then hold their first line at all costs, front-line generals objected to plans to build a second line of German defences two or three thousand yards to the rear.

Despite propaganda from both sides, and a diet of daily casualties from artillery and small-arms fire, the ordinary British soldier had no strong feelings about fighting the Germans, other than to defend himself and the few creature comforts he had made for himself in his maze of dreary trenches. The British mocked their plight in a song imploring military recruiters—it was still a volunteer army—to

> Send out my mother,
> My sister and my brother,
> But for Gawd's sake don't send me.

The French and the Belgians reacted to the war with more emotion than the British. It was being waged on their land, every hectare of which they wanted back. As treaty-bound neutrals, the Belgians had lived under a guarantee of their borders since independence in 1830. The French had lived in an atmosphere of *revanche* since 1870, when

Alsace and Lorraine were seized by the Prussians. (In Paris there was a statue of a young woman swathed in chains, symbolizing Strasbourg.) With that in mind, when Ludwig Renn, a young officer near the front lines at Bertincourt, south of Arras, received orders for his chemical company to go into reserve and rest, his captain quickly had second thoughts. *'Nein,'* he said, recalling Renn to the field telephone. Christmas Eve was approaching. 'The French realize that Christmas is, for the Germans, a great festive day and they might turn that to account precisely this night.'

By 4 December, as wintry rain made movement impossible, the British commander of the 2nd Corps worried about the 'live-and-let-live theory of life' that had surfaced on both sides. Neither side was firing, for example, at mealtimes, and although little fraternization was apparent, unspoken understandings accepted the status quo, and friendly banter echoed across the lines. The 'death and glory principle', as Lieutenant Charles Sorley, a poet, put it, was, in the circumstances, useless. Unannounced, even unspoken, arrangements lessened the discomfort while discouraging the enmity that encouraged the killing. A Royal Engineer, Andrew Todd, wrote to the Edinburgh *Scotsman* that soldiers on both sides, 'only 60 yards apart at one place', had become 'very "pally" with each other'. They were so close that they would throw newspapers, weighted with a stone, across to each other, and sometimes a ration tin, and, Rifleman Leslie Walkinton of the Queen's Westminsters recalled, 'shout remarks to each other, sometimes rude ones, but generally with less venom than a couple of London cabbies after a mild collision'.

On the morning of 19 December, so Lieutenant Geoffrey Heinekey, new to the 2nd Queen's Westminster Rifles, wrote to his mother, 'a most extraordinary thing happened . . . Some Germans came out and held up their hands and began to take in some of their wounded and so we ourselves immediately got out of our trenches and began bringing in our wounded also. The Germans then beckoned to us and a lot of us went over and talked to them and they helped us to bury our dead. This lasted the whole morning and I talked to several of them and I must say they seemed extraordinarily fine men . . . It seemed too ironical for words. There, the night before we had been having a terrific battle and the morning after, there we were smoking their cigarettes and they smoking ours.'

The initiatives for one of the long war's few humane episodes came largely from the invaders, yet not from their generals or their bureaucrats. Leading intellectuals like Rainer Maria Rilke and Thomas Mann had viewed

10

the war as an essential defence against hostile forces representing cultures less rich and technologies less advanced. In *'Fünf Gesänge'* Rilke, the leading lyric poet in the language, celebrated the resurrection of the god of war rather than a symbol of weak-minded peace. In defence of *Kultur*, Mann went to occupied Belgium to observe the future. To be excoriated as Hun barbarians when Germans allegedly represented the higher civilization appeared to him an absurd inversion of values, a feeling shared by educated young officers at the front who came out of professional life. Although war itself might seem necessary for Germany, a wartime Christmas seemed, to many who took the festival seriously, befouled. Captain Rudolf Binding, a Hussar, wrote to his father on 20 December that if he were in authority, he would ban the observance of Christmas 'this year'.

Ordinary soldiers were oblivious to such sensitivities. As Christmas approached, Tommy and Jerry indulged in occasional and undeclared live-and-let-live cessations of fire. Jeers were swapped where the trenches were close enough to permit it—*'Engländer!'* one side would shout, 'Jerry!' (or 'Fritz!') the other. Most exchanges were in English, for many Germans had lived and worked across the Channel, some as waiters in hotels or seaside resorts, others as cooks, cabbies and even barbers, all summoned home in the last, hectic, prewar days late in July. So many Germans were allegedly working in England before the war that at a House of Lords debate a speaker charged that 80,000 German waiters remained as a secret army awaiting a signal to seize strategic points. P. G. Wodehouse satirized such nonsense in *The Swoop! Or How Clarence Saved England,* about a Boy Scout who perceives, in the sporting results in his newspaper, a secret code to alert the Germans. Few readers were amused.

So much interchange had occurred across the line by early December that Brigadier General G. T. Forrestier-Walker, chief of staff to Sir Horace Smith-Dorrien of II Corps, issued a directive unequivocally forbidding fraternization, 'for it discourages initiative in commanders, and destroys the offensive spirit in all ranks . . . . Friendly intercourse with the enemy, unofficial armistices and the exchange of tobacco and other comforts, however tempting and occasionally amusing they may be, are absolutely prohibited.'

Tempting they were. In World War I, creature comforts were cherished even more than comradeship and unit loyalties. The serving soldier's idea of high civilization was a warm, dry place; the opportunity to satisfy the stomach and the bladder, and sleep. Both commands had warned against fraternization, for incidents unrelated to the season had already been reported. Such violations likely to erode discipline, General Erich von Falkenhayn warned, were to be 'investigated carefully by superiors and discouraged most energetically'. It was difficult, however, to feel belligerent behind muddy earthworks or from a flooded trench. The Flanders mud, Captain Valentine Williams of the Irish Guards remembered, 'was greasy and glutinous around Ypres, chalk-white and slimy but no less sticky to the south'. There was 'no stone anywhere in the region', and a few hours of rain churned up 'a rich layer of creamy, foamy mud that absorbs water like a sponge and never gives it up'. An expanse of squalid, isolated farms at best, intersected by ditches and canals and dotted with poplars and polder willows before artillery fire had obliterated most of them, Flanders was prey to bitter winds from the North Sea, and icy rain. Yet even stalemate exacted a price. There were always more dead and dying sprawled inaccessibly between the lines, the result of raids across No Man's Land to assess enemy strength and to take a prisoner for interrogation. Still, a shift in mood was quietly creeping over the desolation, in part because a disproportionate number of German units were now undertrained and unenthusiastic Bavarian, Saxon, Hessian and Westphalian reservists, rather than elite Prussian professionals, many of whom were deployed on the Eastern Front to keep their own homelands from the Russians. Once the Czar's armies were defeated, the German command planned to bring most of its Prussian divisions westward by rail to overwhelm the French, and what British remained. Dismayed by early casualties, the War Office in London considered withdrawing all but a token force to protect the Channel coast—a defeatist prospect to which British generals in France objected.

Most higher-ups had looked the other way when scattered fraternization occurred earlier. A Christmas truce, however, was another matter. Any slackening in the action during Christmas week might undermine whatever sacrificial spirit there was among troops who lacked ideological fervour. Despite the efforts of propagandists, German reservists evidenced little hate. Urged to despise the Germans, Tommies saw no compelling national interest in retrieving French and Belgian crossroads and cabbage patches. Rather, both sides fought as soldiers fought in most wars—for survival, and to protect the men who had become extended family.

To prevent deadlock, British commanders began mounting, in mid-December, a series of small although costly attacks on German positions intended to provoke aggressive responses. The most expensive failure, at Ploegsteert Wood—'Plugstreet' to soldiers in the field—on 18 December, resulted in massive casualties, including many from poorly directed friendly artillery fire. Many of the dead remained unburied, some literally impaled on enemy barbed wire, a rueful song already much too familiar conceding the realities:

> If you want to find the old battalion,
> I know where they are . . .
> They're hanging on the old barbed wire.

Private Henry Williamson remembered seeing some of their graves after the war, including one, under a Star of David rather than a cross, reading 'R. Barnett. The Rifle Brigade. Stoke Newington. Age 15.' The misdirected lyddite shells had been imported from prewar Germany.

As the Germans prepared for the holiday, bringing up small trees and holiday provisions, Rudolf Binding was not appeased by what he labelled the 'Christmas gift stunt'. Promoted by newspapers, commercial enterprises packaged *Liebesgaben,* or loving gifts. One advertisement showed two comfortable officers sitting by opened boxes of *Weihnachtspakete,* and behind them a small Christmas tree on an ammunition box decorated with a holly wreath. No trench was visible. At the front, as real *Weihnachtsbäume* were emplaced, the troops, especially the Saxons, attempted to decorate them, no easy matter in

15

trench conditions, although the weather was becoming more Christmaslike. Rain was giving way to frost, but beyond both banks of the flooded Lys, the fields were covered by shallow ponds that were treacherous at night.

The British were making very different Christmas preparations. Recalling the success of Queen Victoria's brass chocolate box for Boer War troops in 1899, a prized acquisition embossed on the lid with her royal profile, the government-sponsored but privately financed Princess Mary's Sailors' and Soldiers' Christmas Fund replicated the gift. Everywhere that men (and 1500 nurses) wore the King's uniforms, the services shipped a packet in the name of George V's daughter, Princess Mary. The small oblong box contained cigarettes, pipe tobacco and a greeting card in the King's script, 'May God protect you and bring you home safe'. A non-smoker's tin of sweets was also prepared, and special ones for Indian troops—altogether 2,166,008 boxes. Plum puddings were sent by the *Daily Mail,* chocolates from Cadbury, butterscotch from Callard & Bowser. For fifteen shillings, an advertisement in British papers promised, one could send a soldier at the front a thousand Gold Flake cigarettes, or for only nine shillings a thousand Woodbines, each with a Christmas card.

The plethora guaranteed that even the few possibly overlooked received something. 'I am keeping well,' rifleman Percy H. Jones wrote home on the 24th, 'in spite of the large number of Christmas parcels received.' In what was left of Belgium, its troops received a royal bounty of King Albert cigars and Queen Elizabeth mufflers. Mobilized by their government to organize private giving, Frenchwomen had issued a call for *Noël du soldat* donations. At a time when a man wasn't considered a warrior unless he smoked, and when the act of incinerating tobacco and ingesting smoke filled the monotony of waiting, which was much of war, or blotted out fear, which was the rest of war, Christmas gifts at the front often meant either the implements of smoking or the product to be smoked away. The surplus impossible to stuff in a knapsack, store in a muddy trench or consume, created some of the impetus for exchanges, often disproportionate ones, and even with the enemy.

Military deliveries were suspended for twenty-four hours in order to bring forward 355,000 Princess Mary tins, which a Grenadier Guards major complained were 'a positive nuisance'. In his diary G. D. Jeffreys complained that it was 'rather ridiculous to hold up rations and ammunition when, after all, our first business is to beat the Germans. Our enemy thinks of war, and nothing else, whilst we must mix it up with plum puddings.' That Major Jeffreys was mistaken seems evident if one accepts even a fraction of such reports from the front as appeared in the *Jenaer Volksblatt*. The 'semi-official' dispatch, A Christmas Onslaught onto the Field-Grey [Troops]', was the witless sort of soldier humour palatable when one's side is winning:

> Yesterday about four-o'clock in the afternoon there was a fierce and terrible onslaught of Christmas packages onto our trenches. No man was spared. However, not a single package fell into the hands of the French. In the confusion, one soldier suffered the impaling of a salami two inches in diameter straight into his stomach . . . Another had two large raisins from an exploding pastry fly directly into his eyes . . . A third man had the great misfortune of having a full bottle of cognac fly into his mouth.

One German soldier, realizing that in their comfortless trenches such gifts were mere *Weihnachtspakete* to men without a *Mädel* to deliver them at the traditional *Bescherung* ceremony on Christmas Eve, wrote a plaintive '*Notschrei aus den Argonnen* to his hometown newspaper:

> I wear love's gloves on my hands,
> Love's leggings warm my thighs,

Love's tobacco fills love's pipe,
In the mornings I wash with love's soap.
For loving gifts, a thank-you letter:
Warm is love's cap against my skull;
I sigh to myself, 'So much love—and no
  girl!'

The *Kaiserliche* equivalent to the Princess
Mary box was, for the ranks, a large
meerschaum pipe with the profile of Crown
Prince Friedrich Wilhelm on the bowl, or a box
of cigars inscribed *Weihnacht im Feld, 1914*.
Noncommissioned officers got a wooden cigar
case inscribed *Flammenschwert*—a flaming
sword. *Liebesgaben* by public subscription were
more generous. Dominik Richert, a young
infantryman who marked his Christmas at
Vendin-le-Vieil, near Armentières, noted
that his *Pakete* included '*Schokolade,
Zuckerbrötchen, Bonbons, Zigarren, Zigaretten,
Dauerwurst, Ölsardinen, Pfeifen, Hosenträger,
Halstücher, Handschuhe ünd so weiter.*' Such
openhandedness relieved any guilt feelings
at home about shops that were bursting
with Christmas prosperity. With wartime
constraints not yet pinching, it was a splendid
holiday season across Germany and Austria—
but for the absence of Fritz. And it was no less
a wonderful Christmas in England, despite the
unfortunate absence of Tommy.
  In his diary on the 23rd Captain Gerald
Burgoyne of the 4th Royal Irish Rifles, south

of Ypres, noted that his company, a rabble—
'a regular mob, shockingly disreputable'—
assembled by an indifferent recruiting officer,
would not get its plum puddings 'until we
return for them'. Some battalions had their
issue in advance, and his sergeant-major
complained that the area was 'littered with
lumps of plum pudding simply chucked away.
It's pearls before swine to try to treat some
men as human beings.' In snow and sleet they
were preparing to move into the trenches near
Kemmel, to do '24 hours in the fire trenches,
24 hours in the Support [trenches], and 24
hours in the Reserve'.

Concerned with their own preparations for
the holiday, each side did not forget their
counterparts, physically close though in a
different world. Despite what Captain J. L.
Jack of the Scottish Rifles called the 'yellow
porridge' which made movement difficult, as
Christmas approached, friendly approaches
from both lines increased. On balance a hard
frost seemed a worthwhile Christmas wish.

The wretchedness in which men struggled
to exist had already stirred brief and
localized pre-holiday truces. A week before
Christmas near Armentières, a *Daily Express*
correspondent wrote later, the Germans
slipped a 'splendid' chocolate cake into the
British lines with a message explaining, 'We
propose having a concert tonight as it is our
Captain's birthday, and we cordially invite you

to attend—provided you will give us your word of honour as guests that you agree to cease all hostilities between 7:30 and 8:30 . . . When you see us light the candles and footlights at the edge of our trench at 7:30 sharp you can safely put your heads above your trenches, and we shall do the same, and begin the concert.'

The invitation was accepted with an offer of tobacco, and at the appointed hour a 'double quartet' of whiskered heads popped up and sang 'like Christy Minstrels'. Opposite, the British applauded each song, and a 'big voice' responded from the German parapets, 'Blease come mit us into the chorus.' After a killjoy on the British side shouted back, 'We'd rather die than sing German,' the big voice boomed, in English, 'it would kill us if you did.' And with an emotionally sung *'Die Wacht am Rhein'* the trench footlights went out. A few shots deliberately aimed at the heavy clouds ended one of the precursors to the Christmas truce.

On the sector facing the kilted 2nd Cameronians, who were bailing cold, muddy water from their trenches, the Germans on the morning of the 23rd began risking exposure in the open, waving outstretched arms to show they were without weapons. When a lieutenant in the Cameronians, Malcolm Kennedy, shouted for instructions, his company commander, Captain E. B. Ferrers, shouted back, 'Don't shoot, but count them!' The Scots suspected a ruse to slip someone past to survey

21

their positions for a night raid. Also on the 23rd, the company of Berkshires on their left, Kennedy recalled, relaxed suspicions enough to allow 'a couple of Germans to come across'. In English, a 'friendly exchange of cigars and verbal greetings' followed, and one of the Germans remarked 'that he hoped the war would end soon, as he wanted to return to his former job as a taxi-driver in Birmingham'.

That afternoon, as a light snow fell, the 16th Bavarian Reserve Regiment, replaced in the mud by the 17th, moved into the ruins of the monastery at Messines (Mesen), halfway between Ypres and Lille. Since every room above ground had been shattered by their own shelling earlier in the war, when they had advanced as far as the Marne, troops set up a *Weihnachtsbaum* in the cellar and began bringing in the 'agreeable libation' sent by breweries as far off as Munich. After nightfall on the 23rd, according to *Vize-Feldwebel* Lange of XIX Corps, Saxons from Leipzig began placing small Christmas trees on the parapets of their trenches, replete with candles affixed by clamps. Their sector was quiet. Lange, the equivalent to a British staff sergeant, watched Tommies crawl out of their trenches, curiosity rather than courage involved, to ask about the glittering trees which had materialized on the bare, blasted landscape. Although fraternizing was a court-martial offence on both sides, company officers pretended not to notice.

Lange's men explained to the Berkshires that the *Tannenbaum* was more important than the war. Nothing would keep them from celebrating Christmas Eve among their festive trees. (They had been transported to the front by the thousands.) Soon the Tommies were back with word that two of their own officers were waiting just beyond the German barbed wire to speak with Lange's major. With an impromptu cease-fire holding, both sides agreed on an informal truce in their area for Christmas Eve, and Christmas Day.

With the sparkling trees came trust that the enemy opposite was serious about a respite from war, however ugly the setting and whatever might follow an inevitable return to hostilities. A single *Tannenbaum* on a parapet might be an unexplainable anomaly. Emerging rows of them were something else.

Unknowing, but aware of earlier stand-downs, the *Manchester Guardian* the next day editorialized shrewdly,

It will be strange if one of those truces arranged tacitly by the men and winked at by the commanders does not occur tonight in order that, if possible, the Germans may find something to take the place of Christmas trees and the English something to take the place of holly in the trenches . . . Tomorrow, too, the [message] boards which have been in use for signalling 'hits' on either side will very likely bear more or less chaffing greetings. For the longer [that] troops lie over against one another in trenches the more there grows up a certain friendly interest. This, however, does not interfere with the business of fighting.

It would interfere, and in one aspect the *Guardian*'s visionary writer was already wrong: the efficient Germans had their trees.

Concerned about the implications of fraternization, especially Christmas cease-fires, which could have a disproportionate emotional resonance, the British High Command, from St Omer, 27 miles behind the trenches, issued a Christmas Eve warning: 'It is thought possible that the enemy may be contemplating an attack during Xmas or New Year. Special vigilance will be maintained during this period.'

Although both sides seemed reluctant to fire, hidden snipers, seemingly beholden to nothing but their vocation, assured a certain level of wariness. That morning Rifleman A. R. Bassingham of the 5th London Rifles, standing too tall, took a shot to the head. The British had, as yet, no helmets. Formerly a tenor in a music hall group in civilian life, he had been counted upon for Christmas carolling. Instead, recalled Graham Williams, he was collected by stretcher-bearers after

24

dark—a reminder that Christmas was also for killing.

Late that afternoon at St Yvon above Plugstreet Wood, Lieutenant Charles Bruce Bairnsfather, twenty-six, an engineer and 1st Warwickshires reservist (and the trench cartoonist of future 'Old Bill' fame), watched the sun dip below a clear sky and felt 'a sense of strangeness' in the air. No shooting in his sector had marred the waning daylight. 'It was just the sort of day for peace to be declared,' he thought, wishing for an 'immense siren blowing' to announce something portentous and then for a small figure running toward him who would turn out to be a telegraph boy with a 'wire' from the King. Opening the envelope with trembling fingers, he reads, 'War off, return home.'

No such fantasy materialized, but something unexpected happened nonetheless. 'I came out of my dugout,' he recalled, 'and sloshed along the trench to a dry lump, stood on it and gazed at all the scene around: the stillness, the stars, and the now dark blue sky . . . From where I stood I could see our long line of zigzagging trenches and those of the Germans as well. Songs began to float up from various parts of our line. One of them, "not far away", closed,

If old Jerry shells the trench,
Never mind!
Though the blasted sandbags fly

You have only once to die.
If old Jerry shells the trench,
Never mind!
If you get stuck on the [barbed] wire,
Never mind!
If you get stuck on the wire,
Never mind!
Though the light's as broad as day
When you die they stop your pay.
If you get stuck on the wire,
Never mind!

When the chorus faded into the strange stillness of Christmas Eve it was succeeded by the strains of what seemed a distant mouth organ. Under a pale moon swelling just beyond the quarter and already up in the afternoon to compete with a brilliant red early winter sunset, Bairnsfather took advantage of the quiet to visit a dugout closer to the German line, from which the sounds drifted. There, a knot of Tommies were looking over their parapet as if something was happening which he could not yet see.

'What's up?' he asked.

'The Boches [The disparaging word for Germans was used mainly by officers or to officers. The ranks preferred 'Fritz' or 'Jerry'. *Boche* or *Bosche* was a variant of *caboche,* or head, often used to mean blockhead or the head of a nail.] sir; you can 'ear 'em quite plain. There's a feller over there shoutin' in

26

English, and one of 'em's got a concertina or something.'

From the German trenches, accompanied by an accordion, came the refrains of *'Deutschland über alles'*, then more songs. Shouts rang across the line, then shouts in return. Reproduced memorably decades later in the bitter yet sentimental stage satire *Oh What a Lovely War!,* something unparalleled in the ancient history of warfare was beginning to happen. In an early scene in the play, Tommies hear the Germans singing *'Stille Nacht, heilige Nacht'* and shout, 'Guten singing, Jerry!' The Germans in upstage darkness ask in return for 'a good song for Christmas', but since the Brits do not take the holiday with Dickensian seriousness, a soldier responds with a bawdy services version of a music hall ballad:

> It was Christmas Day in the cookhouse,
> The happiest day of the year.
> Men's hearts were full of gladness
> And their bellies full of beer
> When up spoke Private Shorthouse,
> His face as bold as brass,
> Saying, 'We don't want your Christmas
>   pudding:
> You can stick it up your . . .'

'Tidings of comfort and joy, comfort and joy,' the others chorus. And the song continues, even more bawdily.

'Bravo, Tommy!' echoes from the unseen German trenches, and a Fritz announces that a gift from his side is coming. The British dive for cover, and shout for a sandbag to cover it, but the container, a boot, explodes only with sausages and chocolates. They scurry to find something to return, and one furnishes his Christmas card from Princess Mary, and another 'the old girl's Christmas pudding'. Once the Germans offer 'good Deutsche Schnapps' if the Brits will meet them 'in the middle'. In football terms, a Tommy agrees to 'see you in the penalty area'. And they move out warily to greet each other.

'Stone the crows!' a stage soldier wonders. They were not supposed to be such friendly adversaries. The day had begun much as had every miserable day. The weather on the 24th, however, had suddenly become cold and clear. It had been 'a glorious afternoon', a Field Artillery officer wrote to *The Times* several days later, 'and several aeroplanes were up which were duly shot at by the Germans'.

The 1960s pop hit 'Snoopy's Christmas' imagined the comic strip Snoopy, who dreams atop his kennel of the days he never spent as a flying ace in his Sopwith Camel, in the air that day. Although his wings are icing dangerously, he confronts the dreaded Red Baron, who forces the doughty beagle down. Although the bells below are ringing out Christmas joy,

28

Snoopy is 'certain that this was the end', yet the Red Baron emerges from his cockpit not with a pistol but with a bottle of bubbly, announcing, 'Merry Christmas, mein friend!' The mock-ballad had begun with a lusty chorus of *'O Tannenbaum'*, and it closes well into the tradition of the Christmas truce:

> The Baron then offered a holiday toast,
> And Snoopy, our hero, saluted his host.
> And then with a roar they were both on
>   their way,
> Each knowing they'd meet on some other
>   day.

The reality was not far removed from Snoopy's dream. On Christmas Eve the Royal Flying Corps dropped a padded, brandy-steeped plum pudding on the German airfield at Lille. The next day the Germans responded with a careful air drop of a bottle of rum.

A field artillery captain who wrote to *The Times* after Christmas had gone 'to pass the time of day' on the 24th with a regiment down the road. His battery was pumping shells, 'but it was on a particular place which I could not observe'. Then, at six, to his surprise, 'things went positively dead; there was not a sound. Even our own pet sniper went off duty. As a rule he ... sends what the telephonists call "a good-night kiss" at 9.15.'

Safely, they sat about a fire in the frost until,

at about eleven, 'a very excited Infantry officer came along and told us that all fighting was off, and the men were fraternizing in between the trenches. We had seen lights flashing on the parapets earlier in the evening and there had been a great deal of noise going on. Shouts from the Germans—"You English, why don't you come out?" and our bright knaves had replied with yells of "Waiter!"'

News of the exchanges leaped the dugouts on both sides. Then, in Bairnsfather's section of the line, out of the dusk from across No Man's Land came the invitation, in English, 'Come over here!'

'Come over yerself!'

With such overtures, the Christmas truce began.

CHAPTER TWO

CHRISTMAS EVE

The truce bubbled up from the ranks. Though it was to become so widespread as to impact much of the front, no one was ever certain where and how it had begun. A fictional realization evokes the mood. Opposite the Saxons near Wytschaete and Messines, Henry Williamson's alter ego in *A Fox under My Cloak*, Phillip Maddison, found Christmas Eve to be literally a silent night. His company, under the cover of moonset, was to pick its way across the 'frost-cobbled mud' with posts, rolls of wire, hammers and staples, to edge the line forward a few yards. Under the gleaming stars and with the air sparkling with frost, they walked easily. Although they risked being mowed down by machine-gun fire, Maddison 'rejoiced that he was not afraid'.

Not a sound came from the Germans. The unbelievable became the ordinary, so that they talked as they worked, without caution, while the night passed as in a dream. The moon moved down to the top of the wood behind them; always, it seemed, they had been moving bodilessly with their own shadows.

Sometime in the night Phillip saw what looked like a light on top of a pole put up in the German lines. It was a strange sort of light. It burned almost white, and was absolutely steady. What sort of lantern was it? He did not think much about it; it was part of the strange unreality of the silence of the night, of the silence of the moon in the sky, of the silence of the frost mist . . .

Suddenly there was a short quick cheer from the German lines, *Hoch! Hoch! Hoch!,* and with the others he flinched and crouched, ready to fling himself flat;

but no shot came.

Voices reached them across the dark void of No Man's Land. Then the Scots saw dim figures silhouetted on the German parapet, and about them more lights. With amazement, Maddison realized that a Christmas tree was being set there, and around it were Germans talking and laughing together. *'Hoch! Hoch! Hoch!'* they shouted happily. Having gone from group to group as the fences went up, Lieutenant Thorverton glanced at his watch and said, 'It's eleven o'clock. One more hour, men, then we go back. By Berlin time, it is midnight. A merry Christmas to everyone! I say, that's rather fine, isn't it?' They had begun to hear from the German parapet a rich baritone voice singing *'Stille Nacht, heilige Nacht'*. The voice came across the mist and 'It was all so strange; it was like being in another world, to which he had come through a nightmare; a world finer than the one he had left behind, except for beautiful things like music, and springtime on his bicycle in the country'.

Maddison wondered about not being fired upon; the enemy seemed too preoccupied to notice. He realized, suddenly, that the gummy mud was gone, turned to frost. It seemed wonderful to be able to walk rather than slip, and to feel dry; and on returning to his lines exhausted, to be able to sleep. But he could not doze through to daylight. Awakening in his bunker to unaccustomed quiet, he quickly realized why, and could not return to sleep. He got up to see for himself whether he had imagined it all. In six weeks of stalemate the miserable trenches had become home, even to signposted names recalling Old Blighty [Although 'blighty' was a popular euphemism for a non-threatening but incapacitating wound requiring evacuation to Britain, 'Old Blighty' concealed sentimental feelings about home.] and he went for a walk in the grey near-dawn along 'Princes Street', a nostalgic Edinburgh name given by the various Scots troops who used the maze of trenches. The unfaded lines on the sleeves of Maddison's tunic betrayed former sergeant's stripes; on his cuffs he had drawn with indelible pencil the braid and star of a second lieutenant, the most expendable rank in the services and the reason he now was one. In the lifting haze he came upon 'wooden crosses in rows'. He paused to listen for some vestige of the war that had strangely vanished, but there was none. His eyes closed; he felt himself 'to be a ghost in his own body'.

Maddison's stir of emotion fled with physical unease. His dysentery had come on again, and he searched among the few ragged trees remaining, where ice glistened on shell craters, for a place to squat. The looseness scalded; he felt weak and knew he had to lie

33

down. Returning the way he had come, he filled an empty duffel bag with leaves and tall grass as he went, stooped into the bunker among the still sleeping men, removed his boots and stuffed his feet into the duffel bag. Once more, he fell asleep.

For those like Maddison, excited beyond exhaustion to sleep, the night was filled with sights and sounds too remarkable to credit one's senses, and daylight came too soon. It took a suspension of disbelief to accept the reality that the hateful enemy hungered for *Brüderschaft*. For most British soldiers, the German insistence on celebrating Christmas was a shock after the propaganda about Teutonic bestiality, while the Germans had long dismissed the British as well as the French as soulless and materialistic and incapable of appreciating the festival in the proper spirit. Regarded by the French and British as pagans—even savages—the pragmatic Germans were not expected to risk their lives on behalf of each beloved *Tannenbaum*. Yet when a few were felled by Scroogelike gunfire, the Saxons opposite the Seaforths stubbornly climbed the parapets to set the endangered trees up once more. To those British troops whose concepts of Christmas had been moulded by Charles Dickens, the custom had become their own. To Arthur Conan Doyle, who after the wartime death of his son turned to mysticism and spiritualism, the British and

Germans had found 'a sudden and extraordinary link in that ancient tree worship, long anterior to Christianity, which Saxon tribes had practised in the depths of Germanic forests and still commemorated by their candle-lit firs . . . It was an amazing spectacle, and must arouse bitter thought concerning those high-born conspirators against the peace of the world, who in their mad ambition had hounded such men on to take each other by the throat rather than by the hand.'

As both sides milled about in a frosty mist still slow to fade, the Queen's Westminster Rifles, near Armentières, sent out Rifleman A. J. Philip to meet five Germans who, after singing since daybreak, shouted for someone to arrange a 'you no shoot, we no shoot' day. Armed only with wine, cakes, chocolate and cigarettes, one German gravely saluted and announced in English that he was an officer and a Londoner (he came from Catford, south of Blackheath). Signboards arose up and down the trenches in a variety of shapes. They were usually in English, or—from the Germans—in fractured English. Rightly, the Germans assumed that the other side could not read traditional gothic lettering, and that few English understood spoken German. 'YOU NO FIGHT, WE NO FIGHT' was the most frequently employed German message. Some British units improvised 'MERRY CHRISTMAS' banners and waited for a response. More placards on both sides popped up.

A Belgian who had taken Christmas Eve Communion in the basement of a blasted church was up at dawn, just north of Poperinge, too agitated to sleep, and saw that the Germans had posted 'HAPPY CHRISTMAS' over a parapet. When they observed heads poking up to read it, the Germans emerged, visibly unarmed. Advancing toward the puzzled Belgians, who had hardly been treated benevolently before, the *Boche* sang, then shouted 'Comrades!' Momentarily forgetting their hatred of the invaders, the Belgians put down their rifles.

Up and down No Man's Land the two sides—even the French—were coming together. In the Aisne valley, near Braine, according to the 254th's *Journal de marche et des operations,* 'towards 9 o'clock, a few German soldiers stand above their trenches while signalling. One of them advances up to near our lines'. In such tentative ways, localized truces began. At Foucaucourt, on the Somme, where the 99th Regiment faced the Bavarians, three hundred of the enemy, led by a junior officer, emerged from their trenches unarmed and advanced halfway to the French wire. To a French captain the *Leutnant* explained the Bavarians' reluctance to fight, and for days thereafter a brisk exchange took place in bread, cognac, postcards and newspapers. 'A perfectly trained [German] dog,' the French reported, 'ensures communications between the lines.'

Far to the south, in the area of Mulhouse and Belfort, according to Catholic field chaplain Max Metzger, writing frankly in the *Kölnische Volkszeitung und Handelsblatt,* it had not even been necessary for Christmas to intervene pacifically, for the old enemies 'have been lying across from each other in the trenches for several weeks now without one party doing anything to the other. The French have nothing but old infantry veterans . . . who are glad when the enemy leaves them alone. And the Germans do not attack because they cannot possibly break through here easily since Belfort is right in front of them. Thus a silent contractual agreement.' A few German replacements unaware of the arrangement would fire a few shots, and the French would 'complain'. When the disturbance ceased, Metzger wrote, 'I was able to convince myself of this fact by strolling about on top of the German trenches right in sight of the enemy for hours . . . without there being one shot fired.'

Elsewhere, it was with shared traditions and song that the two sides approached one another. Yuletide carols initiated a tentative courtship that further developed through physical contact and ultimately the sharing of the soldiers' most valued commodities—food and tobacco and such souvenirs as uniform buttons and insignia.

Carrying a Christmas tree with lighted candles, the Herwarth von Bittenfeld 13th Westphalians trudged through the battalion's trenches from company to company. At each, the soldiers sang into the otherwise silent night, and across the gap between the lines, in distant discord 'with the sounds of English carols from the other side'. The German compulsion to carry lighted trees even into enemy fire (which any light might provoke) was wryly rendered by James Krüss, a veteran of a later war who returned to write stories of rare charm. In *Mein Urgrossvater, die Helden, und ich* (My Great-Grandfather, the Heroes, and I) he told, in the voice of a child, a cliché tale purportedly in a schoolbook, 'The Christmas Tree in No Man's Land'. In it, a zealous Westphalian sergeant, Manfred Korn, determines after dark on Christmas Eve to take a *Tannenbaum* topped by a Star of Bethlehem across to the French lines where, opposite them, are Algerian troops, heathens who know nothing of Christmas. Seizing one of their small trees, the courageous Korn,

in spite of the blazing gunfire, jumped out of the trench into the open field. He sprang over the enemy's trench with the Christmas tree in his hands, completely unaware of the deadly bullets whizzing all

38

around him. He carried the Star of Bethlehem, and that was his protection. Yet, as if that were not enough, as Manfred carefully lit the Christmas tree in the enemy trench, the glow of its light fell everywhere, and all shooting ceased.

Profoundly moved, soldiers on both sides gather to celebrate Christmas, while the Germans sing 'Stille Nacht'.

Great-grandfather is sickened by the saccharine homily, and tells the boy 'what really happened', as he had learned it 'from the captain of a tugboat, who was there'. And there may be some truth in his sardonic retelling, for Krüss confided privately that he had been told the story by his uncle Otto, who actually was at the front. Algerian troops did face the Germans on the British right flank, the 45th Division of the *Armée d'Afrique*, which had fought at the Marne to help save Paris in early September. In great-grandfather's tale, 24 December 'meant nothing' to the Algerians, whose faith was Islam. Unaware of a holiday truce elsewhere, they fired at the Germans on Christmas Eve, endangering a determined pastry cook from Berlin, Alfred Kornitzke, who was making marzipan balls, a traditional festive confection, for his company.

'No one can do this to me,' Kornitzke exploded. Seizing a *Weihnachtsbaum* as holy protection, he lifted it high and, still wearing his white baker's cap, ran toward the enemy lines. The Algerians were baffled by the apparition, for the German appeared too crazy to shoot at and too comical to take seriously. Rather,

> they watched him in amazement, until, after a while, the telephones began to ring inside the French trenches . . . Suddenly the Algerians become aware of the cease-fire . . . In the meantime, Alfred Kornitzke . . . did not stop until he was halfway between the lines. There he set the tree down carefully, calmly took some matches . . . he had intended to use for his petroleum stove, and in the frosty, star-filled night, lit the candles, one by one . . . 'Now, you blockheads,' [he shouted], 'now you know what's going on! Merry Christmas!'

An illustration by Rolf Rettich for James Krüss's story of Christmas Eve 1914, imagining the trek of the determined marzipan baker (upper right) across No Man's Land in *My Great-Grandfather, the Heroes, and I* (1967). Furnished to SW by James Krüss.

The enemy fire ceased. Kornitzke stumped back to his lines and to stirring his precious marzipan mixture before an audience of admiring soldiers. After the war, he vowed, he would become a missionary to the heathens, 'For now I know how it's done!'

Also in the Neuve-Chapelle area, opposite the Garhwal Rifles near Givenchy, the 3rd Westphalians claimed to have rejected British overtures to negotiate a holiday respite. The initiatives were at first rebuffed, but both sides wanted it, and a truce materialized. 'On both sides, firing ceases almost totally. In the evening, Christmas trees are lit within the different companies [of the 5th] and placed atop the parapets.' Fighting had ceased partly because the Westphalians were mired in flooded positions they had not been able to drain during the incessant rain in mid-December. It was so hazardous that a company officer had been crushed to death when an inundated dugout collapsed. Cold water had sluiced into the shallow trenches of the hapless Garhwals, downhill from the 16th Westphalians, who were draining their lines into a ditch alongside the Estaires–La Bassée road. Earlier on Christmas Eve a Sappers officer, Lieutenant Robson, had crept forward toward sounds from the pump, in order to direct a mortar round onto it. He was shot and killed, and the Indian Corps mourned the friendly Robson, who had been in the lines with them for a month. (Another officer would silence it.)

Everywhere, Christmas ritual—especially

song—eased the anxiety and fear of initial contact. *Kronprinz* Wilhelm, then commander of the Fifth Army, in the Argonne, below the southern edge of the British front, and largely facing the French, recalled visiting, with opera tenor Walter Kirchhoff, his 'field-grey boys' of the 120th and 124th Württemberg Regiments. (The Crown Prince was all of thirty-two.) Snow covered the ground. The 'dull drone' of mortars and the boom of artillery greeted him, he wrote, as well as the distant clattering of machine-gun fire. Yet 'every dugout had its Christmas tree, and from all directions came the sound of rough men's voices singing our exquisite old Christmas songs'. The Prince had, indeed, brought Kirchhoff, a leading singer with the Berlin Imperial Opera since 1906, with him from his headquarters staff. Kirchhoff had performed for the English before—at Covent Garden in 1913—but never for the French. He went forward into the 130th Württembergers' trenches, but not with the *Kronprinz.* It was too near the line for the Heir's comfort. He distributed his blue boxes of Iron Crosses from a safe distance to the rear. The next day he learned from Kirchhoff that French soldiers on parapets opposite had applauded until he gave them an encore.

After nightfall, as the temperature in the German dugouts dipped to the freezing mark, a lieutenant wryly known to his men as *'der Alte'* (the old man), 19-year-old Walther

42

Stennes, led the 6th Company in Christmas carols, a curious listening experience to the Garhwals. Less strange to them were the lighted trees along the German parapets, for they suggested to the Indians their *Diwali* festival. An autumn Hindu fertility rite dedicated to the goddess Lakshmi, it was celebrated for five days. On the evening of the fourth—the beginning of the new year according to the *Vikrama* calendar— earthenware oil lamps are lighted and set up in rows on the parapets of temples and houses, and set adrift on rivers and streams. (*Diwali* literally means 'a row of lights'.) And much like Christmas, it was a time for visiting, for exchanging gifts, for decorating houses, for feasting and (to encourage luck) gambling. The German winter solstice observances may have reminded the chilled and unhappy Garhwals of home.

To all but a few of the exhausted Indians, the holiday resonated only dimly. Christmas Eve in Flanders seemed very little like India. The British-officered Indian Corps, its major element the Meerut Division, had been battered on the 20th, and its units gradually replaced by General Sir Douglas Haig's I Corps, but the Garhwal Rifles would stay on the line until the 27th. Winter was severe on the Indians, and the Germans more so. 'Do not think that this is war,' a wounded Punjabi explained to a relative in India. 'This is not

43

war. It is the ending of the world.' They had already lost 9579 men; and the Manchesters and the French 142nd Infantry suffered, in coming to their relief on the 20th, 1682 casualties. 'The bullets and cannon-balls come down like snow,' a Sikh wrote home. 'The mud is up to a man's middle. The distance between us and the enemy is fifty paces. Since I have been here the enemy has remained in his trenches and we in ours. Neither side has advanced at all.'

When evening came, opposing troops, Garhwals excepted, called to each other from trench to trench and sang. A French soldier wrote to his mother that after they first met with the enemy, they chorused, each in his own language, *'Á bas la guerre!'*—'Down with the war!' Carl Mühlegg of the 17th Bavarian Regiment recalled, fifty years later, shouting, *'Nie wieder Krieg! Das walte Gott!'*—'No more war! It's what God wants!'

More quietly, in the fictional French village of Loffrande, 17-year-old Private Schlump, in the anonymously published satirical novel by Emil Schulz, sat safely alone on Christmas Eve in the house commandeered as the local occupation office, realizing that, inevitably, 'the trenches lay before him. The rain fell, and the wind clashed the naked branches against each other. His mother had sent him a package. He unpacked the little gifts lovingly and laid them out . . . On every gift his mother had laid little twigs of fir, and the scent of them, mingled with the smell of the cakes which he unpacked, wrapped round his soul and carried him home.' Schlump was looking through the keyhole at his mother and father as they prepared the tree at home. In Loffrande 'a thin rain whispered down' as he examined his gift-wrapped woollen socks, and a picture book about the seasons.

It wasn't always easy to stop the shooting and make way for the holiday. Securing small trees for a front-line parapet usually meant ordering soldiers to temporary rear area depots where *Weihnachtsbäume* had been delivered. Carl Muhlegg, a private at Ypernbogen, near Langenmarck, went to a battalion field kitchen to pick one up. It was, he remembered fifty years later, 'about thirty-two inches tall, [already] nicely decorated and with candles attached to it'. Near Messines he had to cross a kilometre of open field in which he could be seen by the French, silhouetted in the moonlight with his tree. Hostile shots and a 'string of machine-gun fire' failed to deter him. 'After all, I was Father Christmas bearing a decorated tree, although . . . with a gun over my shoulder and a bag of ammunition!' Delivering the prize proved easier. 'I handed the captain the little Christmas tree . . . He lit the candles and wished his soldiers, the German nation and the whole world "Peace according to the message from the angel".'

Toward midnight, firing ceased and soldiers from both sides met halfway between their positions. 'Never,' wrote Muhlegg, 'was I as keenly aware of the insanity of war.'

Private Heinrich Knetschke, according to the inventive humour magazine *Der Brummer* (The Grumbler), secured a *Tannenbaum,* and more, in less orthodox fashion. Explaining how he spent his Christmas, Knetschke [His name suggests *knechtisch*, an adjective for submissive, slavish, servile.] wrote a letter, prefaced by an admittedly wretched poem, to his 'Beloved Anna' from somewhere in Flanders:

> The weather is cold in France.
> Maybe that's why each soldier
> On his post is now longing
> For the room where his girl
> Is just now lighting a Christmas tree.

'All rights preserved!' Knetschke added protectively about his effusion, then suggested that his lines might stir from Anna a sentimental tear. Outpourings beyond his own, he confided, were emerging from the men in his company, 'the reason being that a postal van of love has arrived and in it were lots of different packages with rhymed verses, which all of us are answering now'. He was also sending his poem, Knetschke confessed, to two other ladies whose names and addresses were

46

helpfully inserted in the *Liebesgaben* they had packed. One included a *gereimte Tabakspfeife*—a pipe with a motto round the bowl—and a scarf decorated with 'very beautiful needlepoint' as well as the patriotic slogan 'A CALL IS SOUNDING LIKE A ROLL OF THUNDER!'

'Beloved Anna,' he went on, 'I well believe you are astonished that I am attempting poetry. However, war causes changes which in ordinary times one thinks would be impossible. Or, as the saying goes, *"heute tot, morgen rot!"*' [Knetschke in his usual confusion garbles the proverbial 'heute rot, morgen tot'—here today, gone tomorrow—into 'gone today, here tomorrow'.] Their situation, he confided, which had been perilous when he last wrote, was now excellent. His platoon had been ordered to a forward position which turned out to be 'a very beautiful pavilion' that in better times must have belonged to a marquis, for it included, he was told, a marquee. 'And a hundred metres beyond is a little château, but we didn't move into it because behind it is an outpost of the French.'

Realizing that their relocation had left the company without a *Weihnachtsbaum*, his *Oberleutnant* had suggested, 'Knetschke, we must secure a Christmas tree!' Happily, Knetschke knew exactly where to find one, as in reconnoitring the château at dusk he had observed a beautiful small evergreen growing uselessly near the rear entrance. In a daring foray he slipped back, cut down the tree, and had begun 'a strategic retreat' when he heard loud voices. Emerging from the chateau, raucously singing the *Marseillaise,* were several *poilu*, precariously clutching bottles of red wine. They 'swayed like rocking horses'.

Cradling the tree, Knetschke rushed back in the darkness to report his *Rotwein* find, and the lieutenant 'gathered up six men and with me in the lead marched to the château. Well, you might be expecting joyously that a decisive battle followed. But it's not the case. Rather, we reached the back entrance and entered the ground floor, and could risk a wrong move as we heard the *Marseillaise* still coming from the cellar. That showed us the way to go. As we stood quietly in the dark, a French officer opened the door.'

Although there was no way to escape notice, he 'had such a load on' that he could not tell friend from foe, and (in French) ordered the Germans to 'move out the champagne'. The *Oberleutnant* 'answered that we had come exactly for this purpose, and we entered the wine cellar . . . Their insensibility was obvious. Half of the French outpost was inside, and they were drunk as loons. After this you will surely believe me that we thanked our Maker that we hadn't come any later because the Frogs would have guzzled up everything all by themselves.'

The enemy captain 'extended his French paw to our *Oberleutnant,* upon which a *poilu* wanted to embrace me. I rejected such fraternization but only, beloved Anna, because he was belching so badly. But then we agreed to a truce for the rest of Christmas on the condition that the *Parleyvoozes* would help us carry fifty bottles into *our* pavilion.'

Despite their success, the episode was, Knetschke tried to explain, 'a nice mess'— *'eine schöne Bescherung'* [A pun seems intended. *Bescherung* in one sense meant ceremonial Christmas gift, but colloquially it was 'a nice mess'.]—in which to be on Christmas Eve. Later, back in their own quarters, having left the French to slip fuzzily into unconsciousness, the Germans put candles on their *Tannenbaum* and, inspired by enemy champagne, sang *'Stille Nacht'* in 'voices like oxen'.

Knowledgeable about French culture when under alcoholic inspiration, his commanding officer described their pavilion as 'genuine Louis Kators'. Knetschke, who had never heard of Louis Quatorze or any other French king, rated Kators as 'really some skilful carpenter'. His heart was full. Private Knetschke concluded, perhaps referring to her ancestry rather than her age, 'Beloved Anna! . . . The delicious wine reminds me of you, in that it, too, is of an old vintage.'

The enmity exchanged across much of

the line as Christmas began was in the form of friendly insults. Opposite the 2nd Cameronians nearby, the Germans had kept their guns quiet throughout the day before Christmas. The Clydesiders were scheduled to leave their trenches after dark to return to reserve (and a respite). The Saxons must have learned of it, for they were determined to send their adversaries off in a festive spirit. 'From the trenches opposite,' Lieutenant Malcolm Kennedy recalled, 'the sounds of singing and merry-making' and occasionally the bark of a German could be heard, shouting, 'A happy Christmas to you, Englishmen!'

Irritated at being called 'English', a departing Scot shouted back, 'Same to you, Fritz, but dinna o'er eat yourself wi' they sausages!' As the Cameronians filed out of their trenches in the other direction they exchanged holiday greetings with the Devons, their replacements, and a Saxon brass band played carols from their trenches as the British peaceably changed places.

Perhaps because the men were still in a combative mode, merriment often began as a response to a challenge. So it was with the Highlanders. When dared to sing (so a Seaforth officer wrote home), the Highlanders responded irreverently with 'Who Were You with Last Night?' and 'Tipperary', both sung 'very badly'. One officer recalled it as 'all most irregular but the Peninsular [war against

Napoleon] and other wars will furnish many such examples'. But even he was surprised when 'the enemy . . . played "Home Sweet Home", and "God Save the King", at 2.30 A.M.!' Lieutenant Sir Edward Hulse claimed in a letter to his mother that good will was not his goal when his 2nd Scots Guards 'assaulted' the Germans with carols. From ten o'clock onward, from their trench positions closest to the enemy, about eighty yards away, 'we are going to give the enemy every conceivable song in harmony, from carols to Tipperary . . . Our object will be to [shout] down the now too-familiar strains of *Deutschland über alles* and the *Wacht am Rhein* we hear from their trenches every evening.' They planned to 'make a rare noise'. But the Germans across the line anticipated his barrage with their own Christmas songs, including

Es ist sehr weit zu Tipperary,
Es ist sehr weit zu geh'n . . .

And at one point, to fit the melody where their own language failed them, they turned to French, with *'Adieu Leicester Square'*.

A German sergeant with an Iron Cross suspended from a black and white ribbon and earned, he boasted, for skill in sniping, led his men in a marching tune, and when they finished, Hulse ordered *'The Boys of Bonnie Scotland, where the heather and the bluebells*

51

grow'. They followed with ballads which both sides knew, 'singing everything from *Good King Wenceslaus* down to the ordinary Tommies' song[s], and ended up with *Auld Lang Syne,* which we all, English, Scots, Irish, Prussians, Württembergers, etc., joined in. It was absolutely astounding, and if I had seen it on a cinematograph film I should have sworn that it was faked!' Twenty years later, when Hulse's long letter home was published, a German officer then opposite, Major Thomas of the 15th Westphalians, wrote a rejoinder for the Christmas 1934 number of a German army magazine. It was already nearly two years into the Nazi regime, and Thomas, an instructor at the Infantry School in Dresden, may have intended safeguarding his combative reputation. He was, he recalled, beyond Le Mesnil and Fromelles, west of Lille, when the initiative to fraternize came from the English side—the 'continuous waving of a white flag . . . about 150 yards from our trench'. (The night before, each side had sung at each other.) Soon afterward the enemy troops came forward, 'making [peaceable] signs all the time'. Their concern was to bury the dead. At the orders of his commander, Baron von Blomberg (a cousin of Hitler's Defence Minister), Thomas went out, accompanied by an English-speaking soldier. 'What were we to do?' he now asked. There was no time to ask for instructions from a higher level. 'Major von

B. therefore decided . . . that there should be a local armistice until 1 o'clock in the afternoon, telling the Englishman that their dead must be buried by that time.'

While the enemy troops, 'assisted by our Field Greys', retrieved and buried the dead, Thomas handed Hulse 'a Victoria Cross and letters which had belonged to an English captain . . . who had fallen in our trench in the course of the attack of the 18th December. Touched by this respectful treatment of the belongings of one of his fallen comrades, Sir H. took off his silk scarf and handed it to me as a memento of this Christmas Day in impulsive gratitude.'

Officers up to the rank of colonel were involved from the beginning but kept a low profile. Colonel F. S. Maude of the 14th Brigade 'whilst at work on our front line' in the frost and darkness 'had a talk with a Bavarian officer opposite us, who gave us his card and a tinned ration'. The next morning his troops would sit on their parapets and sing 'God Save the King'.

In war, all front-line soldiers were equal, but in this competition there were (like Kirchhoff) some superstars. A German cornet virtuoso 'who is probably well known' played across the lines, and a French harmonica performer broke the night silence in his sector with *'Stille Nacht',* while a German violinist stood atop his parapet to offer the French Handel's *Largo.*

As a village church bell was heard at midnight, Christmas Eve, a British correspondent reported, it was followed by 'a voice, clear and beautiful, singing *"Minuit, Chrétiens, c'est l'heure solenelle."* [The English version is 'O' Holy Night'.] And who do you think the singer was? Granier of the Paris Opera. The troops, French and German, forgot to fire whilst listening to that wonderful tenor voice.' The Belgian soldiers Aleks and André Deseyne also recalled hearing 'a French soldier with a splendid tenor voice' near the Polygon Wood—singing that left both sides, when he finished, 'awed and dead silent.' It was a hazardous stage, but Victor Granier had been in jeopardy before. He had debuted in 1903 in Rossini's *Guillaume Tell*, where the hero must cleave an apple off his son's head.

That an individual voice could range such distances suggested unusual mobility, the unearthly quiet, and perhaps some sentimental imagination. Nonetheless, throughout the truce, it was much safer to be festive in reserve. In the shell-damaged church at Illies, some of the 3rd Westphalians gathered among their imported trees as light snow sifted through the wrecked roof, and the regimental band accompanied the troops in singing after a priest preached a sermon. In the ruined monastery at Messines, some of the 16th Bavarians gathered in what was left of the cloister for the distribution of gifts, traditional on the day before Christmas but not always possible in the circumstances. A tree was placed to one side, its candles lit, and *Liebesgaben* laid out for distribution. Rupert Frey of the 7th Company recalled that Major Spatling 'stressed in impressive language the significance of the hour and mentioned their loved ones back home'. What was left of the 'high and gloomy monastery walls vanished, and we saw only the sparkling Christmas tree'. The major offered a prayer for fallen comrades, and the men who could squeeze into the cloister sang *'Stille Nacht'*.

Robert de Wilde, a Belgian artillery officer, remembered a midnight Mass in a barn at Pervyse officiated by a lieutenant. The German trenches were within listening distance. 'We had fixed up a sort of makeshift altar; from the nearby village, abandoned and in ruins, we had fetched a few candle-holders, a missal, a pyx, [The vessel in which the consecrated bread of the Eucharist is kept.] an altar-cloth . . . The men sang their carols, carols from their villages . . . Throughout the whole ceremony, the Boches—Bavarian Catholics—did not fire a single shot.' Another pyx, from the destroyed church at Diksmuide, would be returned by the Germans the next day, trailed across the icy Ijser in a net attached to a rope.

Karel Lauwers, a peacetime artist, and a signaller with the Belgian 12th Regiment on the outskirts of Oostkerke, north of Diksmuide, recorded in his diary that from his trench, which had 'frozen well', he heard the Germans singing 'their Christmas songs, and if I had known, I would [have been close enough to] understand'. As he bent around an unusual open fire, as no shots were being fired, 'the wet mist was covering our backs and heels and the whole field as with a white layer'. When daylight came he would do a charcoal sketch of huddled soldiers.

German gestures of peace became contagious, although no one forgot the war. Hugo Klemm of the 133rd Saxon Infantry Regiment recalled being assembled before the church in the village of Pont Rouge, in which they were billeted, to be warned by the company commander that they had to be on the alert on moving into the line. The English might exploit Christmas. Yet his company had already secured two trees, which, with candles lit, they mounted above their parapets. The Saxons also laid fresh planks on the muddy footpaths of the trenches before settling in to celebrate as best they could. Just in case, once darkness set in, Klemm wrote, 'We fired the occasional shot from our outposts to let the enemy know we would not let ourselves be surprised.'

Both to his left and to his right Klemm watched candles being lighted on trees fronting other Saxon trenches. Latecomers were the reserve company of the 133rd led by Lieutenant Johannes Niemann, which had celebrated in advance. Aware that they were to move into the trenches on Christmas Eve, Niemann's men had opened their *Liebesgaben* in their rear area, sharing surplus boxes from home with puzzled villagers. 'Then at darkness we marched forward to the trenches like Father Christmas with parcels hanging from us. All was quiet. No shooting. Little snow. We placed a tiny Christmas tree in our dugout— the company commander, myself, the [other] lieutenant, and the two orderlies. We placed a second lighted tree on the parapet. Then we began to sing our old Christmas songs: *"Stille Nacht, heilige Nacht"* and *"O du fröhliche".*' ['Rejoice, O Christendom', by Johannes Daniel Falk (1829).]

Their singing attracted almost as much attention across No Man's Land as did the lighted trees, which an English soldier described as 'like the footlights of a theatre'. Many units were spellbound, then reacted, as if an audience, with applause. Albert Moren of the 2nd Queen's Regiment, near La Chapelle d'Armentières, remembered many years later that the 'performance' began just after dark. 'It was a beautiful moonlit night, frost on the ground, white almost everywhere; and . . . there was a lot of commotion in the German trenches and then there were those lights—I don't know what they were. And then they sang "Silent Night"—*"Stille Nacht"*. I shall never forget it. It was one of the highlights of my life.'

From across the barbed wire British units shouted for more, and some Germans replied with *'O Tannenbaum'*. Fired from Very signal pistols, appreciative British flares soared up. Too distant at Fleurbaix to see them, the 2nd Bedfordshires, according to Lieutenant Charles Brewer, [Brewer, who became a BBC producer, was the source for Leslie Baily's *Scrapbook for 1914* radio broadcast, a script reconstructing the episode which, when published (1957), may have influenced the truce scene in *Oh What a Lovely War!*] then nineteen, were appreciating the fact that 'for once it wasn't raining'. They could peer out over their top row of 'soddened sandbags' and see in the moonlight the German trenches and barbed wire 'not 100 yards away, across the slimy churned-up morass of No Man's Land. A body or two lay out there. Everything was still, except the occasional tok-a-tok-a-tok of a machine gun. In my own strip of water-logged trench a chilled sentry stamped and beat his mittened hands. Suddenly he saw a group of glistening lights appear on the German parapet.'

'Look out!' he called. 'Keep your perishin' heads down. I bet it's a sniper's trap.' Brewer was fetched from his dugout to have a look. 'I saw that the lights were on a Christmas tree.

Farther along the line I could see more Christmas trees sparkling.' Then his company began to hear, 'splendidly sung', what they could recognize as *Stille Nacht*. They gave the Jerries a cheer; then one of Brewer's chaps shouted, ' 'Ere, let's sing 'em something back! Come on!' And they sang, less artistically but no less heartily, 'We are Fred Karno's Army', irreverently exploiting the tune of the hymn 'The Church's One Foundation' ('. . . is Jesus Christ Our Lord'). The words meant nothing to most Germans. The ex-waiters from Brighton and Blackpool and the ex-cabbies from London and Liverpool, however, knew Fred Karno. Unlike British volunteers, German men were regularly called up in peacetime for compulsory military training. Karno's shambling incompetence was the musichall's answer to Charlie Chaplin. He symbolized the English civilian army of instant and unprofessional soldiers and the cultural and disciplinary gulf between Tommy and Fritz:

We are Fred Karno's army,
The ragtime infantry.
We cannot fight, we cannot shoot,
What earthly use are we?
And when we get to Berlin,
The Kaiser, he will say,
'Hoch, hoch! Mein Gott,
What a bloody fine lot

59

Are the ragtime infantry!'

'I shouted to our enemies,' Captain Josef Sewald of the 17th Bavarians, then twenty-four, recalled, 'that we didn't wish to shoot and that we [should] make a Christmas truce. I said I would come from my side and we could speak with each other. First there was silence, then I shouted once more, invited them, and the British shouted 'No shooting!' Then a man came out of the[ir] trenches and I on my side did the same and so we came together and we shook hands—a bit cautiously!'

The Queen's Westminster Rifles at La Chapelle d'Armentières also assumed that the lights across the line were a ruse, and fired. There was no return fire, which puzzled them more. 'The first unusual thing happened,' rifleman Percy Jones, a 'Saturday night soldier of eighteen', wrote a few days later in his diary, 'when we noticed about three large fires behind enemy lines. This is a place where it is generally madness to strike a match.' When lights began appearing on trench parapets, Jones heard what he thought were 'weird tunes' on bugles and horns, and singing. Suspicious, the Westminsters guessed that the enemy—the 127th Saxon Infantry—was readying an attack,

so we commenced polishing up ammunition and rifles and getting all ready for speedy action. In fact we were about to loose off a few rounds at the biggest light when . . . words were heard (probably through a megaphone), 'Englishmen, Englishmen. Don't shoot. You don't shoot, we don't shoot.' Then followed a remark about Christmas. This was all very well, but we had heard so many yarns about German treachery that we kept a very sharp look-out.

How it happened I don't know, but shortly after this our boys had lights out and the enemy troops were busy singing each other's songs, punctuated with terrific salvos of applause. The scene from my sentry post was hardly creditable. Straight ahead were three large lights, with figures perfectly visible round them. The German trenches, which bent sharply and turned to the rear of our advanced positions, were illuminated with hundred of little lights. Far away to the left, where our lines bent, a few lights showed our A Co[mpany] trenches, where the men were thundering out 'My little Grey Home in the West'.

At the conclusion . . . the Saxons burst into loud cheers and obliged with some German tune. They also sang one of their national airs to the tune of 'God Save the King'. We replied with the Austrian hymn, at which the applause was terrific.

The German national hymn then was '*Heil dir im Siegerkranz*' (like the English anthem, from an eighteenth-century tune), about the victor's crown going to the Kaiser, but Fritz also had an irreverent *Bierhalle* variation, thanking someone—the benefactor depended upon the audience—'for this round' of drinks, and vowing that

> If you pay for one more round
> We will like you twice as much.

It would be sung many times in many places along the front before Christmas was over. The Austrian hymn, which, with variations, echoed the original, had been composed by Franz Josef Haydn, who on a visit to London was so impressed by 'God Save the King' that, returning to Vienna in 1797, he created his own version, which made 'God preserve our noble Emperor' seem almost English, even in German:

Gott erhalte Franz den Kaiser,
Unsren guten Kaiser Franz!

Hoch als Herrscher, hoch als Weiser,
Steht er in des Ruhmes Glanz!

When the song exchanges ceased, Jones wrote, 'some time was spent yelling facetious remarks across the trenches. After this, some daredevils in E Co[mpany] actually went out, met, and shook hands with some of the Germans and exchanged cake and biscuits. As the night went on, things gradually grew quieter.' The first contacts were tentative and timid, and in the darkness the troops slipped back into their own lines. But the lyrics made clear that this day was special, with much to share. Many of the men, and even their officers, took heed.

The 134th Saxons at La Bassée Ville near Warneton, opposite the British at St Yves, had attended Christmas Eve services at dusk in the ruins of a sugar refinery. The regimental band played; a chaplain sermonized; and soldiers sang carols, including the venerable hymn *'Dies ist der Tag, den Gott gemacht'* ('This Is the Day the Lord Has Made'). Lieutenant Kurt Zehmisch of the 134th's 11th Company noted in his diary, 'I have ordered my troops that, if at all avoidable, no shot shall be fired from our side either today on Christmas Eve or on the two pursuant Christmas holidays. Hardly have we occupied the trenches both we and the English find ourselves trying to attract the other side's attention.'

At first the Saxons whistled; then they shouted in English, their efforts lost in the blasts of 'insane' shooting from the 106th Regiment from Leipzig, whose troops were deliberately sabotaging the efforts of the 134th. But Zehmisch's English and that of two of his men, Möckel and Huss, managed to break through, and soldiers on both sides slipped from the wire to meet in a 'willow ditch'. One Englishman, his arms raised to show he was weaponless, held in one elevated hand a cap, bottom up and brimming with cigarettes to exchange.

Both sides shouted challenges and impertinences across the lines, punctuated by yells and applause. 'Then we placed even more candles than before on top of our trenches, which were about a kilometre in length . . . We sang all sorts of Christmas songs as well as folk songs from and about home, and from our village quarters [to the rear] the tunes of our band carried clearly through the starry night.' Each time the Saxons placed a lighted Christmas tree on their parapets, the English shouted approval. 'Like most of my men,' Zehmisch wrote, 'I stayed awake the entire night. And it was a wonderful night.'

How the initiatives arose, and how they were received, differed from unit to unit across the variegated geography of Flanders. A weary sentry in the 13th London Regiment of the 8th Division, often called 'Princess Louise's' and sometimes 'The Kensingtons', [The sculptress daughter of Queen Victoria lived on until 1939 at Kensington Palace.] looking out toward the German lines, reported that the enemy trenches were 'all alight'. As more candles were lit—the supplies shipped in were enormous—other sentries took up the cry, and watchful troops peered over their parapets. Few shots were fired, each ignored by the other side.

'English soldiers! English soldiers!' challenged the German voices. 'Happy Christmas! Where are your Christmas trees?' And songs pulsating with thumping energy grew louder opposite the Kensingtons. Across from the 6th Gordons, the Germans, realizing that their neighbours were Scots, altered their invitation to 'No shoot tonight! Sing tonight! Jock! Sing tonight!'

The regimental history of the Kensingtons conceded, 'We were a little embarrassed by this sudden comradeship, and, as a lasting joke against us, let it be said that the order was given to stand to arms. But we did not fire, for the battalion on our right, the Royal Irish Fusiliers, with their national sense of humour, answered the enemy's salutations with songs and jokes and made appointments in No Man's Land for Christmas Day. We felt small and subdued and spent the remainder of Christmas Eve in watching the lights flicker and fade on the Christmas trees in their trenches and in hearing the[ir] voices grow fainter and eventually cease.' Nearby, the 1st Devonshires took their chances when the Germans offered, as elsewhere, 'You no shoot, we no shoot'.

Almost always, it was the Germans who at

least indirectly invited the truce. They were winning, and had much less to lose by it. Christmas may also have meant more to the Germans. And as they celebrated vigorously and without apparent concern, the other side gave in to its war weariness. The Germans, too, were weary of a war they were assured would be short.

For a soldier identifying himself only as 'Rudolph', a Christmas spent at war was still war. He wrote frankly to the Berlin *Vorwärts* that his best Christmas gift was learning that his unit would be transferred after eight weeks 'up to our knees in water' to occupation duty in Brussels. But during their last three days of trenches duty in the slime, even they had tried forgetting themselves in song. Once they had 'set up housekeeping', one of Rudolph's comrades had produced a harmonica from a dry pocket. They began singing *'Heilige Nacht'* as if all was well. 'After the third stanza, as we take a look over the parapet across to the English, we notice that they hearken to us attentively.' One battalion stood on its earthworks, cheered and waved its hats. Not only were the London Rifles attentive, according to W. R. M. Percy, who had left Prudential Assurance in Holborn to volunteer, 'The singing and playing continued all night, and the next day our fellows paid a visit to the German trenches, and they did likewise.'

Such men had marched off to their

promised six-weeks' war singing patriotic anthems and chalking exuberantly on their troop trains *'Ausflug nach Paris. Auf wiedersehen auf dem Boulevard'*—'Excursion to Paris. See you again on the Boulevard'. However much enemy territory they occupied, winter had come there, and they were bogged down well short of victory. Christmas helped— at least for the moment—to forget that, and to bring together men who really, they recognized, didn't hate each other. Their fraternization, dangerously unwarlike from the headquarters perspective, seemed unstoppable.

Captain Valentine Williams of the Irish Guards recalled, below 'clouds of tobacco smoke mounting in the sparkling air', exchanging wry jokes about the war. The first seven years would be the worst, a Tommy averred, but Fritz insisted that the war would end soon, contending, 'England *kaputt!*' The English were 'gently sarcastic' about the failure of the German fleet to emerge and give battle, and the Germans changed the subject to the failures of the Russians on the Eastern Front. But when retorts warmed, both sides again turned to unargumentative song.

CHAPTER THREE

THE DEAD

In the darkness of Christmas Eve it was possible to celebrate the phenomenon of light in the German candlelit trees and what the British called electric torches. But daylight exposed the casualties beyond the barbed wire—none of them pretty and many already putrefying. By night they had been stumbled upon; by day they inhibited any festive rapprochement. The dead could not be put out of mind—every combatant was a potential corpse—but they could be put out of sight. No Man's Land would become a vast burial ground.

When Henry Williamson's Phillip Maddison awoke that morning, his boots were caked with white, and frozen hard. Getting his feet back into them was agony; walking in them was worse. The sun was breaking through the mist, and to the rear of the trenches, mail was being distributed. He sat on an unopened crate of two-ounce tobacco tins, read his letters, and opened a Christmas packet from his father that contained a two-ounce tin of Capstan. After making a fire to fry his breakfast bacon and boil water for tea, he opened another gift—his brass Princess Mary box, which he decided to send home to his mother as a souvenir, with all its contents. He had no need for any of it.

Nearby was a village, still stubbornly inhabited. Maddison walked toward it through a wood. First he encountered a shell-shattered château, its roof collapsed above weakened red-brick walls, its masonry shattered and grounds perforated by ice-filled craters. Risking fire, he walked around the tumbled bricks to the back. A smashed door looked uninviting, but he wriggled through. The first room, he discovered, had been used in all four corners as a latrine. The kitchen was cluttered with fallen plaster, broken crockery and pots, and upset tables and chairs. Beyond was a wooden stairway. Although the stillness suggested that the floor above was also abandoned, the hair at the nape of his neck twitched as he climbed, crackling the fallen ceiling plaster underfoot. The upstairs corridor was bare but for dead bees lying shrunken on the broad, gouged floor planks. A bedroom door was splintered open; a dead German in grey uniform lay behind it, the back of his head smashed.

Another dead German lay on the bed, his body decomposing and swollen. Letters had fallen out of his tunic; Maddison recognized the curious gothic lettering he found difficult to read, but he pocketed them anyway. Then he opened his knife and sliced two buttons from the corpse for souvenirs at the very time that in the field the British and Germans were warmly trading uniform buttons. The crown and the W (for Wilhelm) intrigued him, but as he held them closer to examine them, the reek of death on his fingers made him retch with nausea. The officers (as they appeared to be) seemed to have been dead for six or seven weeks, ever since the fighting near Ypres had stalemated; and his heart raced as he thought of his own fallen friends who would look like that now if still unburied.

Slipping outside, chilled in the wan sunlight, he rubbed his hands in the mud and melting ice in a crater, drying them on tall weeds. Fingering for a cigarette, he tried smoking the obstinate odour away. Noticing an undamaged outhouse and needing again to relieve himself, he sat above the pan, straining and fearing the scalding.

An abandoned bicycle with obsolete hard tyres lay against the outside wall. Once emptied, Maddison pushed the rusty bike out and pedalled to the village, where he revisited a seedy bistro which its *propriétaire* stubbornly kept going. Warming wet boots by the fire, he ordered an omelette and white wine, marvelling that such civilized amenities survived. Eating hurriedly, he understood that he had better return before he was missed.

The artillery officer who later wrote to *The Times* had arranged to cross toward the

70

German trenches after breakfast, to a location where the wire entanglements about which the war now seemed limited were only seventy to eighty yards apart. Even his colonel, he reported, an anomaly among the upper ranks, 'came out to see the fun . . . You can hardly imagine it; the only sentries were two unarmed ones . . . All our fellows were digging [graves] in the open and theirs were doing the same.' Once the dead were interred out of sight, friendly gestures from the living seemed appropriate. It was one thing to sing or shout across the lines, but the darkness concealed sprawled and decaying corpses, as did Maddison's shattered house.

To maintain amity, the combatants had agreed almost everywhere on Christmas Eve (although neither side stuck strictly to it) that 'the only thing forbidden was to make any improvement to the barbed wire'. Further, they concurred 'that if by any mischance a single shot were fired, it was not to be taken as an act of war, and that an apology would be accepted; also that firing would not be opened without due warning on both sides'. For a moment in time the war restored rules evoking an earlier century and a less complicated world.

'Finally,' the artilleryman wrote, 'we all walked out and one of their officers came to meet us. We all saluted, shook hands, and exchanged cigarettes.' To go beyond the language of gesture required breaking an unforeseen barrier. Most Germans spoke little English and less French, and the British 'could not muster a word of German between us'. Anxiety arose about what to do next. Helpfully, the Germans plucked a private out of the trenches who had lived 'some years' in America. Inflated with his new importance, he interpreted enthusiastically for both sides. The officers with him 'were little more than boys, and one of them had already been wounded. They were intensely polite and there was any amount of clicking of heels'. As it seemed vital to somehow underrate the army that had nearly swept to Paris in the first weeks of the war, the artillery officer added that the men in the German ranks whom he saw were also 'rather young' yet 'not despondent or underfed'—curious language since the Germans were not only winning but well provisioned. Some, he observed, were 'shy of uniforms', a questionable assumption since the enemy was comfortably outfitted. Perhaps, like Lieutenant Hulse, they were not wearing full uniform in the miserable trench conditions, although Hulse's Scots doggedly wore their kilts. A German officer extracted a photograph of himself in uniform and asked to have it posted to his sister in Liverpool—the extraordinary was becoming ordinary.

A letter published in the *Frankfurter Zeitung* viewed the truce with the French differently.

Between their trenches the mingling was spurred by 'daredevils' from both sides who went over the barbed wire unarmed, 'and walked towards each other until suddenly a shot fired somewhere off to the side caused everyone to disappear immediately'. Then 'the whole show started all over again', and 'an extensive trade began' between the lines, close enough to the enemy side that 'the view of the French trenches revealed that they were not covered and that the dugouts were somewhat back . . . It was good that newspapers were exchanged . . . The French knew that the Russians were not doing well at all. Some were even of the correct opinion that they merely were England's errand boys, the main culprit behind the war.' To make that point, the Germans offered, in exchange for the *Echo de Paris,* copies of the *Lustigen Blätter* and the *Kladderadatsch* 'replete with a few good caricatures of the English'. Unfortunately, the officer reported, 'the enemy artillery is not yet in as peaceful a mood as the infantry'. Soon after, the over-friendly division was prohibited from further fraternization.

Although both sides exploited the truce to negotiate the disposal of casualties, it also became an unspoken opening for what followed. Amid the flickering candles on Christmas Eve, for example, a German officer from the 15th Westphalians shouted to Lieutenant Harold de Buriatti, in English, 'I want to arrange to bury the dead. Will someone come out to me?'

Taking three men from his Bedfordshires, and a lantern, Buriatti met four unarmed Germans and their lieutenant, who credited his good English to a stay in Canada and holidays in Brighton. He knew, he explained, as others in other sectors did, of twenty-four of their dead between the lines. Could they have leave to bury them after daylight? The British offered to take the request to higher authority. Earnestly, the Westphalian wound off his signet ring and gave it to Buriatti. Another company of the Irish, acknowledging the chivalry of the Germans in permitting the collection of twenty dead, killed in a futile attack the week before, sent a gift from their subaltern's Christmas box. In return the German captain sent something of his own. The next day, working side by side, the British and the Germans would dig the graves. It was more a beginning than an end.

In daylight, Christmas cheer was inhibited by the decaying shapes of the dead, some mercifully covered by new snow. 'So in the grey light of dawn,' Klemm wrote, 'our platoon commander Lieutenant Grosse met an English officer and agreed to bury the dead between the two lines if the higher authorities gave their assent.' In the darkness the night before, the English lieutenant had warily directed fire against the emerging parapet Christmas trees.

Soon few would care about higher authority.

'We gravely saluted each other,' a lieutenant on the other side recalled, 'and I then pointed to nine dead Germans lying in midfield and suggested burying them, which both sides proceeded to do. We gave them some wooden crosses . . . which completely won them over, and soon the men were on the best of terms and laughing.' Several Saxons 'spoke very fair English, and some hailed from London, much to our cockneys' delight, and talk became general about "Peecadeely".' The chatter evaded deeper emotions. Disturbing a fetid corpse was agonizing duty. Some had fought side by side with the dead men, or had come from the same towns and villages. Most men moved out into No Man's Land with feelings too mixed to define.

As the curious Westminsters trudged toward the enemy lines they found them, unseen before from the shallow sight angles of the parapets. Germans stood in dense masses atop their own trenches awaiting them, and between the lines a flooded ditch about four feet wide divided the unploughed field over which they had been fighting. Crossing with difficulty, Percy Jones discovered to his shock that it was 'simply packed with dead Germans. Their faces, brown and leather-like, with deep sunken cheeks, and eyebrows frozen stiff, stared up horribly through the clear water.' In the field through which the ditch cut, Tommies were already laid out for burial. A lieutenant looked over the 'dreadful ranks' for familiar faces, although deterioration made recognition difficult. 'They lay stiffly in contorted attitudes, dirty with frozen mud and powdered with rime.'

Up and down the line the retrieval of corpses and their burial were tacit preconditions for fraternization. Opposite to the 1st North Staffordshires, where Captain R. J. Armes had arranged his area's cease-fire, a German burial party left its lines after reveille and was joined by British volunteers. Across from the 2nd Bedfordshires, a German officer accompanied by two unarmed men left their lines with a white flag to request a cease-fire for burying his dead. It was 10:00 A.M. The Bedfordshires longed to move into the open, but remained ordered to their trenches. Less confined, Germans unassigned to the digging party sat on their parapets watching the grisly work.

At Ploegsteert, the appeal came from the other direction. The 1st Somerset Light Infantry asked the Germans opposite for permission to remove the British dead to a rear-area cemetery. After a brief ceremony the bodies of three officers and eighteen other ranks were carried off. Up and down the line in Flanders, Christmas morning would be marked by religious observances marking birth and death.

Near the Sailly-Fromelles road west of Lille, the chaplain of the 6th Gordon Highlanders, J. Esslemont Adams, an Aberdeen minister, wanted to exploit the pause to bury Scots Guards killed after their failed attack a week earlier. The Gordons had taken their positions. Also, a Gordons casualty lay between the lines, a victim of sniper fire on Christmas Eve. Accompanying Lieutenant Colonel Charles McLean, the battalion commander, through the trenches, Adams saw each side, exposed, gazing curiously across, then men climbing out and greeting the enemy. McLean warned his men back, but none paid any attention. A soldier brushing past explained that the Germans were acting 'peacefully'. In fact a German patrol had encountered a British scout before dawn while on an errand to the lines opposite. Armed with a bottle of schnapps, they offered the Highlander a drink and a promise that if his side continued the informal truce, they wouldn't fire either.

With the message relayed, no shots greeted a German party which had come at dawn to the British wire, and there was, Stephen Graham wrote, 'a general exchange of souvenirs, and much mirth'. Mustering their limited English, the Germans conceded that they were tired of battle and exasperated with harsh discipline, but thought the war would be over soon once Russia and France sued for peace. Abandoning McLean, Adams strode off toward a ditch that marked the line. Holding his arms raised as he walked, he called out to the Germans, 'I want to speak to your commanding officer. Does anyone speak English?'

'Yes!' said one. 'Come over the ditch.'

Now close enough to be identifiable as a minister, Adams hurried forward and saluted, but as he began to explain, a rabbit, once secure among the abandoned cabbages, darted out. Instantly, all formalities vanished. Both Germans and kilt-flying Scots gave chase, and the Germans caught the trophy. 'It was all like a football match,' a soldier in the 6th Gordons wrote, 'the hare being the football, the grey tunicked Germans the one side, and the kilted "Jocks" the other. The game was won by the German who captured the prize. But more was secured than a hare—a sudden friendship had been struck up, the truce of God had been called, and for the rest of Christmas Day not a shot was fired along our section.' ['The football imagery in the rabbit chase is from 'One Day of Peace at the Front', *Daily Mail*, 1 January 1915.]

Following the commotion, the chaplain and the German *Oberstleutnant* settled upon a joint service in No Man's Land. Adams would open with the 23rd Psalm, and prayers would follow from both sides in English and German.

Intermingled, the dead lay in the sixty yards

between their lines. Soldiers went out to identify the bodies, carrying the Germans to one side, the British to the other. Before the sun was high, the digging had begun. The British brought over wooden crosses made from biscuit boxes for both sides. If the shooting resumed, they would be contending through the crosses and the graves.

'Why did you and the German commander take your hats off to one another?' a soldier asked Adams afterward. He explained that the German had taken out his cigar case and offered a cigar. 'May I be allowed not to smoke,' asked the abstemious Adams, 'but to keep this as a souvenir of Christmas here and of meeting you on Christmas Day?'

'Oh, yes,' said the German with a laugh, 'but can't you give *me* a souvenir?' Adams dug into the lining of his cap for a copy of 'The Soldier's Prayer'. He had kept it since the war began. Many soldiers' prayers survive, some from Cromwell's time. One carried in 1914 included the lines, 'Shield us, in danger's hour . . . Hear my prayer for [my] Comrades in this great war, incline their hearts to think of Thee. Keep the Officers who lead us; help us all to render them cheerful obedience.' And it went on to exhort enduring 'hardness', 'suffering', and 'death' as 'good soldiers of Jesus Christ'. Removing his own hat, the *Oberstleutnant* put the slip in it. 'I value this because I believe what it says,' he assured Adams, 'and when the war is over I shall take it out and give it as a keepsake to my youngest child.'

The curious Highlander had still another question: 'What was in the notebook the German commander showed you?'

Adams said that he had been shown the name and address of a Scots subaltern who had died in German hands and was buried in the graveyard at Fromelles, at the church on the hill. In the aftermath of the failed attack, the *Oberstleutant* had realized that the young officer, who lay beyond medical aid, was struggling to get something out of a tunic pocket. The German bent to help, and saw it was a photograph of the dying man's wife. 'I held it before him, and he lay looking at it till he died a few minutes after.' The chaplain took down the name and address to write to the widow.

To the south of the Gordons, Captain Giles Loder of the 2nd Scots Guards walked a half-mile to negotiate the retrieval of other Scots fallen in the same raid, close to the enemy barbed wire. An 'extremely pleasant and superior brand of German officer' arranged to have Loder's twenty-nine dead also brought to 'the halfway line'. Loder himself took on the 'heartrending' task of collecting identity discs, paybooks and personal effects from the bodies, often from 'chaps one knew so well, and who had started out in such good spirits on December 18th.' Many were shattered from high-velocity fire at close range. Their rifles still lay nearby, but Christmas goodwill ceased there. Any weapons beyond midpoint of the line, the Germans insisted, were spoils of war.

From a French-speaking officer, the Scots learned that two of their lieutenants who had been badly wounded and evacuated by the Germans had died in a rear-area hospital and were also buried at Fromelles. Already the site of military cemeteries that would expand enormously, Flanders was stirring with impromptu committal ceremonies. Some burials would be isolated and perfunctory, as Captain Josef Sewald of the 17th Bavarian Regiment recalled. As the enemies milled about in No Man's Land south of Lille, an English lieutenant, apparently Charles Brewer, approached Sewald to ask whether his men could bury a soldier killed the day before. At dawn, Brewer's men, seeing several Germans atop their parapet, had picked their way through the wire and 'solemnly shook hands', gazing at each other 'almost shyly. So here were the fellows we had been sitting opposite for two months—the fellows whose slightest visible movement had meant the pressure of a trigger.' Sewald had said, 'Why not?' And 'they brought the dead man, laid him on the ground, and we all laid a handful of earth upon him and together prayed the Lord's Prayer:

Vater unser, der du bist im Himmel,

Geheiligt werde dein Name.

About a hundred bodies lay about Chaplain Adams. The pale moon, waxing beyond the quarter and bloated as it lifted over the flat horizon, had risen just after noon, contributing to the strangeness of the moment. A lieutenant aged 19 in the 6th Gordons, Arthur Pelham-Burn, who hoped to study for the ministry after the war, wrote to a friend from public school days at Lancing that the mass burying was 'awful, too awful to describe so I won't attempt it', but the joint burial service was 'most wonderful'. According to Pelham-Burn, Adams 'arranged the prayers and [the twenty-third] psalm etc and an interpreter wrote them out in German. They were read first by our Padre and then in German [*"Der Herr ist mein Hirte . . ."*] by a boy who was studying for the ministry. It was an extraordinary and most wonderful sight. The Germans formed up on one side, the English on the other, the officers standing in front, every head bared. Yes, I think it was a sight one will never see again.'

Breaking the silence, Adams saluted the German lieutenant colonel. They shook hands and said their farewells. The men returned to their lines. (Lieutenant Hulse identified the enemy units as the 158th Infantry Regiment and 11th *Jäger* Battalion of the 25th Westphalian Brigade—'the men we had attacked on the night of the 18th. Hence the feeling of temporary friendship, I suppose.') In his battalion's war diary Captain Loder wrote, 'Both sides have played the game'—a common expression that fortnight. Yet a private in the Gordons, Alexander Runcie, remembered that while returning from the burial an unsentimental soldier showed him a dagger he had concealed and added, 'I don't trust these bastards.' One did not have to mistrust the enemy to recognize that German Intelligence—like his own side—sent out night patrols, hoping to seize a prisoner for questioning, and was using the truce to peer past the barbed wire.

Near Neuve-Chapelle, Lieutenant Colonel Lothian Nicholson, commanding the 2nd East Lancashires, discovered on Christmas morning that the enemy troops opposite had erected several small trees on their parapets overnight and had begun shouting, 'Merry Christmas, East Lancs!' In his diary he noted, 'Pretty smart, considering that it was our first tour in this line.' As he was consulting with an Engineers officer about the vulnerability of his low-lying trenches to flooding, Nicholson began to notice 'a lot of men hobnobbing with the Hun in No Man's Land'. It was too late to stop them. He went out, too,

and found [H. N.] Fryer, one of our attached subalterns, talking fluent German to a German NCO. I gathered

83

that they wanted leave to bury the dead of which there were a good many lying in No Man's Land. After vain endeavours to get hold of a German officer I sent the German NCO with a message to the B[attalio]n Commander that he could have an hour and a half & that we would bury all the dead lying close to our line & they could do the same with theirs. This was accepted and subsequently extended for another hour in the course of which we buried all the dead & Sanders went out from the Adv[ance] Post in the 3rd Sector & recovered the body of Dilworth, a Sher[wood] For[ester] who had been killed about a month before.

No patrol had located Dilworth, evidence of how long and how thoroughly that *Stellungskriege*—stalemate—had existed, not only in Flanders but all along the front from the North Sea to Switzerland. Some bodies—hardly pretty to begin with but now gruesome—had been sprawled in No Man's Land since October. Stalemate was hardly the condition where the *poilu* patrolled the line. The French in the southernmost reaches had made little progress, and almost everywhere south of Flanders the front languished within post-1870 frontiers. Desire to fight was low in the mud and flood of autumn, and nonexistent in the snow and ice of winter. Boots, hooves, and wheels alike bogged down. The exhortations of distant generals burning with desire to recover Alsace and Lorraine meant nothing.

Despite the seeming taboo about fraternization on the French side, the war diaries of many units reveal much more of it than did official communiqués. According to the Christmas report of the 56th Brigade, at Cappy, in Picardy, 'The day is quiet. A completely spontaneous truce establishes itself along the entire sector of the front, notably at the two extremities where French and German soldiers come out of their trenches in places to exchange newspapers and cigarettes.'

The records of the 12th, 15th, and 20th Bavarian regiments along the Somme mention tacit truces with other French regiments—the 20th, 22nd, 30th, 32nd, 43rd, 52nd, 99th, 132nd, 137th, 142nd, 162nd, 172nd, and 254th. The cease-fire was spreading, although quietly and with less trust than with the British. Government censors ordered French newspapers, even the English-language *Paris Tribune,* to ignore the unwelcome reality, and *Le Matin* (apparently prompted by officialdom) would declare that any soldier found 'guilty of holding conversation with the enemy would be court-martialled and shot for treason'. But few *poilu* read *Le Matin,* and one soldier drew a revealing cartoon of a squad of Frenchmen clambering over (and perhaps squabbling over) a monster German meerschaum pipe, captioning it 'The gifts of Noel 1914. One [pipe] per battery?'

'The gifts of Noel 1914. One per battery?' An anonymous pen-and-ink sketch by a French soldier satirising the attractions to the enemy of the German gift meerschaum. The drawing was found by the Germans on 22 April 1915, on the body of the apparent cartoonist. In Flanders Fields Museum, Ypres, Belgium.

There was no way to conceal French fraternization, even when reporters were muzzled, as sick and wounded *poilu* evacuated to rear-area hospitals related excitedly what little they knew. Probably commissioned to write an implicit contradiction, Maurice Donnay would publish, on 31 December 1914, an article, *'La Sainte Haine'* (The Sacred Hate), on the front page of *Le Figaro*, which began, 'No German can open his mouth or take up his pen without lying'. Still, stories emerged from the front after Christmas and an official pamphlet, *La Vie de Tranchée* (Life in the Trenches), would appear early in the new year to claim that only the Germans and British sang across the lines. Yet, once the enemy shouted, approvingly, *'wunder schon!'* and 'these pigs' chorused back across No Man's Land, 'You should hear the sounds that greet them: dogs, cats, tigers! . . . Their voices are drowned out [by the British], with lots of vigorous cries of "Shut up!" as well.' And the belligerent insults allegedly impelled the Germans to open up with gunfire.

To the north, the French 29th *Regiment d'Infanterie* reluctantly agreed to a truce just long enough to bury the dead. 'The meeting was an awkward one,' Émile Barraud wrote, 'as the French came out with shovels while the Germans brought cigars. After a French corporal had shaken hands with a German, salutes and cigars were exchanged, the bodies collected and buried, the men returned [to their lines] in silence, and in the evening firing began again.' According to Charles Toussaint, a bicycle messenger in the 74th Regiment, after a night when the enemies sang to each other, a German soldier bearing a 'white napkin' walked across the line at daybreak to announce that his side 'had decided to call a truce for Christmas Day and asked for reciprocity'. The French readily agreed and a 'village fair' ensued between the trenches, with convivial exchanges of gifts from Christmas packages.

As the bartering gained momentum, Toussaint, awaiting instructions at regimental headquarters, heard Lieutenant Colonel Brenot angrily telephone forward, 'If they don't want to go back, fire over their heads!' Toussaint hurried to an observation post to see for himself, and found No Man's Land, usually deserted, dramatically 'peopled with all these men who wanted to forget the war, at least on Christmas Day'. But he added to his diary a concern that 'we might have ended up losing sight' of 'discipline and its requirements'. Not Brenot, however, who ordered warning shells fired by their 75s, their fuses timed to explode 'high enough to avoid wounding our boys'. (Obviously they were also set to avoid the friendly enemy.) The Germans understood, and the fraternization continued, if more cautiously, into the night.

A Mannheim newspaper put a different spin on French fraternization, publishing a postcard then reprinted by the *New York Herald,* about a suggestion from the other side that the dead in No Man's Land be interred. 'There was general handshaking; the dead were buried; cigars, cigarettes and newspapers were exchanged and a general celebration ensued. Then the Frenchmen suggested that we shoot no longer, [and] promised that they themselves would not resume hostilities in that event. But they added, "Beat those Britishers. We have no use for them." Well, we gladly agreed to this. Again there was handshaking, arms were resumed, and everybody crawled back to his trench.' No paper in Britain carried the incendiary story.

Overt unfriendliness on the command level surfaced in the sector in Picardy where the

56th Brigade first reported 'a completely spontaneous truce along the whole front'. More revenge-minded than his troops, the French division commander planned to take advantage of the fraternization he deplored, and ordered explosives laid to thwart an attack he claimed to expect from the allegedly devious Germans. Sappers exploited the quiet to lay 800 kilos of powder close to the most forward enemy trench—perhaps the most un-Christmas-like action of the day. But with Christian charity the French decided not to set it off until eleven, which, given Berlin time an hour later, would be, at midnight, the close of the enemy Christmas.

Even the French Foreign Legion, the least pacific of soldiery, dug in awkwardly at an abandoned turnip field between Frise and Éclusier, became involved in the truce. The night before, Private Victor Chapman, 25, son of the American critic John Jay Chapman, wrote home, cajoling shouts from the Germans led the Legionnaires to shout back *'Boches!'* The Germans tried *'bon camarade'*, then 'cigarettes', and finally *'Nous boirons champagne à Paris'*. In the morning the Germans began again, and a Russian Legionnaire who spoke German offered the greetings of the season. A *Boche* retorted 'that instead of nice wishes' they would be grateful if the French buried their compatriot who had lain between the trenches for two months.

'The Russian walked out to see if it were so, returned to the line with a French officer and a truce was established. The burying [and] funeral performed, a German Colonel distributed cigars and cigarettes and another German officer took a picture of the group.'

A half-mile down the line, Chapman saw none of the ceremonies, 'though our Lieutenant attended. No shooting was interchanged all day.'

After the carolling and hesitant fraternization of the night before, the men in the burial parties, once enemies and certain to be so again, were prompted to sombre reflection. The war had already been brutal and deadly, but likely to go on. Yet when the soldiers on both sides were not spading fallen comrades into alien soil, they were coming together in ways so unpredictable and extraordinary that they felt compelled to write in disbelief to families and to newspapers still largely uncensored about what they had seen and done.

Henry Williamson remained tormented ever afterwards by the failure of one soldier then unknown to history to step forward in a burial party or to mingle with his comrades and their new friends. 'Three weeks after my eighteenth birthday,' Phillip Maddison's creator wrote as himself, 'I was talking to Germans with beards and khaki-covered *Pickelhauben,* and smoking new china gift-pipes glazed with the Crown

Prince's portrait in colour, in a turnip field amidst dead cows, and English and German corpses frozen stiff. The new world, for me, was germinated from that fraternization. Adolf Hitler was one of those "opposite numbers" in long field-grey coats.' Later, in the pacifist futility of the 1930s, Williamson would write hopefully that Hitler's wartime experience and the warm rapprochement in his sector might coalesce in memory to stave off another war, but Hitler had never welcomed the truce or such utopian dreaming.

To escape Austrian conscription in 1913, Hitler had slipped into Bavaria, where, earlier, he had eked out a living painting postcard scenes. From Munich, on the day the Germans invaded Belgium, he volunteered for duty, and eight weeks later was in Flanders as a *Feldegänger*—field messenger—with the 16th Bavarian Reserve Infantry Regiment. In *Mein Kampf* Hitler would write, 'A single worry tormented me at that time, as with so many others, would we not reach the Front too late?'

In a fierce exchange with the French near Wytschaete, his company commander was gravely wounded, and Hitler dragged Captain Hoffman under fire into their own lines. Hoffman would die of his wounds, but Corporal Hitler, a gaunt, sallow soldier with a thick, dark moustache and hooded eyes, received from Kaiser Wilhelm himself on one of his rear-area inspections of battle-weary

91

troops, the Iron Cross, Second Class. It was, Hitler recalled, 'the happiest day of my life'.

Although he was out of the line in reserve, discussion arose about crossing into *Niemandsland* to share Christmas with the British. He refused. 'Such a thing should not happen in wartime,' Hitler argued. 'Have you no German sense of honour left at all?' More than patriotic scruples were involved. Although a baptized Catholic, he rejected every vestige of religious observance while his unit marked the day in the cellar of the Messines monastery to which they had retired on the 23rd. 'Adi' was distinctly odd. He received no mail or parcels, never spoke of family or friends, neither smoked nor drank, and often brooded alone in his dugout. In the ruins open to the sky, Corporal Frobenius, a Lutheran theology student also decorated with the Iron Cross, read the Christmas gospel to a joint congregation of Catholics and Protestants, but not to Corporal Hitler.

In another ruin the night before, a very different kind of reading had taken place, emphasizing the dead more than the living. At a *'tannenbefränzten Altar'* in an unnamed village church in Flanders also wrecked by shelling and with blood-spattered walls, soldiers of the 50th Regiment had listened to a *Weihnachtsmärchen*—Christmas Fable—of extravagant Wagnerian mawkishness read by its author, a fellow *Landser.* Walter Flex, 27, an enlisted volunteer with a Ph.D. who had been a tutor in the Bismarck family, assured the rapt men through his piously occult tale that 'on Christmas Night the dead talk in human voices'. For inspiration he had carried with him into the line his three sacred books, a New Testament, a volume of Goethe and Nietzsche's *Also sprach Zarathustra,* but his sentimental homily suggested a medieval fable as sweetened by Sunday School.

A young mother is widowed in a war of an earlier time that has threatened Germany from east and west. She cannot maintain her rented farm and is turned out by the rich landowner and forced to wander in the woods with her young son. In despair she drowns herself and the child in an icy lake, awakening to an unearthly light and guided by a stern, solemn soldier who takes her to a subterranean place where dead heroes, a community of the elect, oversee souls yet unborn. She sees such souls in the form of children playing at a lake formed of the tears of soldiers' wives and their offspring, and emitting a rosy glow. Songs about the miraculous birth in Bethlehem are heard, and Flex likens the war dead to the angels who brought the news of Jesus to the shepherds in the fields. Escorted in an instant to the centre of the earth, she encounters, enthroned, a godlike soldier with sword and orb in his hands, attuned to the sounds of the world above. When any disharmony vibrates the mystical sword, a deceased soldier is sent above to eradicate the threat to peace on earth. Each day a different demigod is seated as *Führer,* and on her entrance she discovers the leader for the day is her own dead husband. He gives her a chalice of wine and a shell heaped with wafers, and instructs her to feed herself and their son. She soon sleeps.

It is midday when she awakens and discovers that she is in the snow at the edge of the lake in which she had drowned. She and the child are alive. The food and drink offered below remain with them, renewing themselves magically. Nearby the heartless *Grundbesitzer* reappears, now metamorphosed into benevolence by a visit from one of the angelic fallen soldiers. The landlord grants her the farmhouse from which she had been evicted, leading her and the boy across the threshold himself. The bread and wine continue to renew themselves as a holy inheritance.

Although Flex's eerie romance evoked the quasi-religious cult of death that may have removed some dread from his regimental *Kamaraden,* he never published his Christmas homily. Commissioned as a lieutenant and shifted by troop train to the Eastern Front, he died in an attack on the Baltic island of Osel (Saaremaa). Suffused with patriotic fervour and published posthumously in 1917, his unfinished autobiographical novel, *Wanderer*

Between Two Worlds, evoked the cult of youth and suggested latent homosexuality, and made his reputation. When the Second World War began, his cloying Christmas tale seemed appropriate for Hitler's regime to resurrect. It was published, followed by many printings, in Munich, with woodcuts that combined Third Reich imagery with period *Pickelhauben.*

In Vienna the Christmas issue of the leading newspaper, the *Neue Freie Presse,* had appeared with a rhapsodic poem, *'Weihnachtsgrüsse'*—Christmas Greeting—by the most popular lyric poet of Wilhelminian Germany, Richard Dehmel, who at fifty-one had volunteered for active army service. He had already celebrated the war extravagantly as *'die grosse Gottesstunde'*—the great hour of God. In *'Weihnachtsgrüsse'* he compared the sound of machine guns to *'Sphärenmusik'*—the music of the spheres. Less lyrically, British soldiers in the trenches called German heavy artillery shells 'coalboxes'. Few fell anywhere along the line on Christmas Day. That was exactly the way that Gustav Riebensahm, commanding a Westphalian regiment opposite Hulse's Scots Guards, wanted it. Christmas had begun in the unearthly quiet of silent guns and a sudden freeze in what he described as 'a hoarfrost of magic and beauty'. As the day waned and the dead disappeared from No Man's Land he added to his diary, 'One had to look again and again to believe what was happening, given everything that had occurred earlier.'

CHAPTER FOUR

OUR FRIENDS, THE ENEMY

In the first hours of the truce, Private W. J. Quinton of the 2nd Bedfordshires recalled hearing the Germans sing 'Annie Laurie' in 'perfect English, and we were spellbound'. When his side applauded enthusiastically he thought of his schoolboy reading of Macaulay:

> E'en the ranks of Tuscany
> Could scarce forbear to cheer.

As the Bedfordshires shouted 'Encore! Good old Fritz!' an approaching German called out warily into the darkness, 'I am a lieutenant! Gentlemen, my life is in your hands, for I am out of my trench and walking towards you. Will one of your officers come out and meet me half-way?' A subaltern appealed to the company commander, 'Let me go, Sir . . . It's a fair offer.' The Bedfordshires' captain suspected trickery. Then, coming closer, the German asked again, 'Will not one of you come out and meet me[?] . . . I am half-way across now, alone and unarmed.' They began to make out a shadowy figure who must have realized how many rifles were pointed toward him.

'Gentlemen,' he entreated, 'I am waiting!'

The Bedfordshires' officer, known to his men as 'Waddy', broke out beyond his own barbed wire and went on. From the other side, the singing grew louder; lights flickered atop the *Weihnachtsbäume* that had delayed ammunition replenishment for days. The enemies met in No Man's Land.

A die-hard lieutenant in the London Rifles recalled sourly that the German trenches looked 'like the Thames on Henley Regatta night . . . I was all for not allowing the blighters to enjoy themselves, especially as they had killed one of our men that afternoon. But my [new] captain (who hadn't seen our wounded going mad and slowly dying outside the German trenches on the Aisne) wouldn't let me shoot; however I soon had an excuse, as one of the Germans,' he claimed, 'fired at us, so I quickly lined up my platoon and had those Christmas-trees down and out.'

The breach in the tacit truce had failed to undermine it. In other sectors the number of unarmed men who were exposed on both sides by morning light soon became vast, including the two officers on the right flank of the die-hard infantry officer. 'Without saying a word to anybody,' he objected, '[they] got out . . . and walked halfway to the German trench, and

97

were met by two German officers and talked away quite civilly and actually shook hands! It was an awfully stupid thing to do . . . but our captains are new, and not having seen the Germans in their true light yet, apparently won't believe the stories of their treachery and brutality.'

To the Germans, the few vocally belligerent Englishmen confirmed what they already believed—that the term *barbarian*, applied to them by enemy propaganda, belonged by rights to the other side. To the Germans a rare civilized Englishman they encountered was Captain R. J. Armes, a broadly moustached Regular in the 1st North Staffordshires on the line just below La Chapelle d'Armentières. He had 'just been through one of the most extraordinary scenes imaginable', Armes wrote to his wife just before dawn:

> I was in my dugout reading a paper and the mail was being dished out. It was reported that the Germans had lighted their trenches up all along the front. We had been calling to one another for some time Xmas wishes and other things. I went out and they shouted 'no shooting' and then somehow the scene became a peaceful one. All our men got out of the trenches and sat on the parapet, the Germans did the same, and they talked to one another in English and broken

98

English. I got on top of the trench and talked German and asked them to sing a German *Volkslied*, which they did, then our men sang quite well and each side clapped and cheered the other.

I asked a German who sang a solo to sing one of Schumann's songs, so he sang 'The Two Grenadiers' splendidly. Our men were a good audience and really enjoyed his singing.

Very likely the Staffordshires missed the irony of the German choice. Some French (defending to the south) would have been less appreciative. Heine's lyrics described two of Napoleon's grenadiers 'who hung their heads in shame' after their defeat and capture, deploring that France 'was lost forever'. After the song, Armes, with another officer, walked across the line and chatted with the German commander. One of his men

introduced us properly; he asked my name and then presented me to his officer ... We agreed to have no shooting until 12 midnight tomorrow. We talked together; 10 or more Germans gathered round. I was almost in their lines within a yard or so . . . Then we wished one another good night and a good night's rest, and a happy Xmas and parted with a salute. I got back to the trench. The

Germans sang *'Die Wacht am Rhein'* . . .
Then our men sang quite well 'Christians
Awake', it sounded so well, and with a
good night we all got back into our
trenches. It was a curious scene, a lovely
moonlit night, the German trenches with
small lights on them, and the men on
both sides gathered in groups on the
parapets.

At times we heard the guns in the
distance and an occasional rifle shot. I
can hear them now, but about us is
absolute quiet. I allowed one or two men
to go out and meet a German halfway.
They exchanged cigars or smokes, and
talked. The officer I spoke to hopes we
shall do the same on New Year's Day. I
said, 'Yes, if I am here.' I felt I must sit
down and write the story of this Xmas
Eve before I went to lie down. Of course
no precautions are relaxed, but I think
they mean to play the game. All the
same, I think I shall be awake all night so
as to be on the safe side. It is weird to
think that tomorrow night we shall be at
it hard again. If one gets through this
show it will be an Xmas time to live in
one's memory.

To the north of Ploegsteert Wood the Seaforth
Highlanders were fraternizing more openly.
The Germans had invited the Scots, who had

been singing carols, out of the trenches and sang Christmas songs back at them. 'I don't think we were so harmonious as the Germans,' conceded Corporal John Ferguson. A German shouted,

'Komradd, Onglees Komradd.' . . . I answered him, 'Hello! Fritz' (We call them all Fritz). 'Do you want any tobacco?' he asks. 'Yes.' 'Come halfways.' . . . We shouted back and forward until Old Fritz clambered out of the trench, and accompanied by three others of my section we went out to meet him . . . 'Make for the light,' he calls, and as we came nearer we saw he had his flash lamp in his hand, putting it in and out to guide us.

We shook hands, wished each other a Merry Xmas, and were soon conversing as if we had known each other for years. We were in front of their wire entanglements and surrounded by Germans—Fritz and I in the centre talking, and Fritz occasionally translating to his friends what I was saying. We stood inside the circle like streetcorner orators.

Soon most of our company . . . hearing that I and some others had gone out, followed us; they called me 'Fergie' in the Regiment, and to find out where I was in the darkness they kept calling out

'Fergie'. The Germans, thinking it was an English greeting, answered 'Fergie'. What a sight—little groups of Germans and British extending almost the length of our front! Out of the darkness we could hear laughter and see lighted matches . . . Where they couldn't talk the language they were making themselves understood by signs, and everyone seemed to be getting on nicely. Here we were laughing and chatting to men whom only a few hours before we were trying to kill!

Even after the extraordinary Christmas Eve, soldiers were astonished by what they saw at daylight on Christmas Day. 'I awoke at dawn,' Bruce Bairnsfather recalled, 'and on emerging on all fours from my dugout, became aware that the trench was practically empty. I stood upright in the mud and looked over the parapet. No Man's Land was full of clusters . . . of khaki and grey . . . pleasantly chatting together.' To Bryan Latham of the London Rifles, No Man's Land 'had the appearance of a football pitch at half-time'.

For his famous cartoons of trench life, Bairnsfather had type-cast the men Latham saw into 'Old Bill', 'Bert' and 'Alf'. 'Old Bill' wore a greatcoat 'that looked as if rats had dined off the bottom, a huge muffler, a balaclava woollen helmet with a battered khaki hat perched on the top, and fingerless gloves'.

Even more unmilitary was Bill's paunchy, bleary-eyed, unshaven face. All three, and their like, were out fraternizing on Christmas morning, as was the case now throughout much of Flanders.

With Bert and Alf and a few others, Old Bill had gathered about several Germans, listening to conversations that were largely unintelligible. 'What a damn silly language!' said Bill uncomprehendingly.

'Sounds like they're gargling,' said Bert.

Happily, many Germans could cope with English. None Bairnsfather saw were armed, and on both sides there seemed to be a 'total lack of suspicion'. The Germans, he concluded loyally, did not look as happy as the English, but they were 'cleaner and dryer'. As on the British side, before any higher-ups 'could quite realize the situation and take the necessary steps of discipline to insure a continuous state of war', the war had taken a holiday.

As a junior officer, Bairnsfather knew only what was happening immediately around him. The High Command knew less. Soon after daylight, puzzling reports came to Field Marshal Sir John French at B.E.F. headquarters out of listening range that unarmed German soldiers (like the fictional Kornitzke) were 'running from the German trenches across to ours, holding Christmas trees above their heads'. They were achieving success 'of a limited kind'. French knew fewer facts than his subalterns but acted nonetheless. According to his diary, he 'issued immediate orders to prevent any recurrence of such conduct, and called the local commanders to strict account', which resulted, he understated later, 'in a good deal of trouble'. Few officers complied, because their men were already out, and even fewer believed that French's prohibitions could be enforced. It is difficult to imagine what field officers could have done, if they had actually wanted to do anything, to arrest the momentum of the truce. Come Christmas morning, most troops on both sides of the line, it seemed, were eager to see it happen.

At the 'earliest crack of dawn' Lieutenant Rudolf Zehmisch of the 134th Saxons wished 'a good morning' to the English opposite. The next section in his battalion had heard of his 'incredible adventure' by field phone and began making 'friendly overtures'. Zehmisch had 'delightful conversations in English, French and German' with enemy officers who had joined him. Contagion had set in. On Christmas morning at Houplines, near Armentières, Frank Richards and his friends in the 2nd Royal Welch Fusiliers 'stuck up a board' on which they had lettered 'A MERRY CHRISTMAS' and waited to see what would happen. (He was used to evading orders. In the ranks since 1901, with duty in Burma and India, he had 'risen', he wrote in a memoir, to private.) When their message was not riddled by fire, two men in his company jumped onto the parapet of their trench and raised their hands above their heads to show that they had no weapons. Two Germans opposite did the same, and began walking toward them, up from the Lys riverbank. As they met and shook hands, the trenches emptied and men on both sides began running toward each other. 'Buffalo Bill' Stockwell, Richards's company commander, had seen it too late to matter, rushing into the forward trench only when his men were gone. His nickname had come from his habit of pulling out his revolver and threatening to blow a man's 'ruddy brains out' for some trifling thing—and what he saw then was no trifle.

Since no choice existed but to accept reality, 'company officers climbed out too . . . Their officers were also now out . . . We mucked in all day with one another'. One English-speaking Saxon confided that he was fed up with the war, and Richards and his friends readily agreed.

Other unit commanders attempted at the start to put limits on fraternization, but were usually no more effective than Buffalo Bill. A belligerent Welch captain hoped to limit the cease-fire, but a sergeant with different views hoisted a large screen lettered 'A MERRY CHRISTMAS'. At first, in the thick ground fog that accompanied the overnight frost, the

Germans failed to see it. Yet, with no shots to fear, men ate their breakfasts openly. As the mist began lifting, soldiers on both sides 'got a bit venturous and looked over the top', normally unsafe in daylight. 'A German started to walk down the tow-path [of the Lys] toward our lines and,' Richards wrote, 'Ike Sawyer went to meet him. The German handed over a box of cigars. Later the Germans came boldly out of their trenches, but our men were [still] forbidden to leave theirs, so they threw out tins of bully [beef], and plum-and-apple jam.' And they shouted, 'Here you are, you poor hungry bastards!'

Exchanges of food were driven by the vast differentials between supply and demand that the holiday had created. Germans would have given much for the legendary coarse English marmalade, but the only jam that reached the troops in 1914 was cheap plum-and-apple, and, weary of it, Tommies would chorus,

Plum and Apple,
Apple and Plum . . .
The A.S.C. [The Army Service Corps, the
    supply and transport arm, had first
    crack at rations it hauled.] get
    strawberry jam
And lashings of rum,
But we poor blokes,
Only get Apple and Plum.

From the German standpoint the surfeit was a boon. In exchange—in Richards's sector—they promised to roll toward the British lines two barrels of beer. In Captain Stockwell's account, the Saxons opposite 'had been shouting across in English' all Christmas morning but only when the fog had lifted did his troops see half a dozen of the enemy standing on their parapets without arms, shouting, 'Don't shoot. We don't want to fight today. We will send you some beer.' Three of them began to roll a barrel that had been hoisted onto a parapet 'into the middle of No Man's Land'. More Saxons emerged between the lines and

Things were getting a bit thick. My men were getting a bit excited . . . We did not like to fire as they were all unarmed, but we had strict orders and someone might have fired, so I climbed over the parapet and shouted, in my best German, for the opposing Captain to appear . . . We met and formally saluted. He introduced himself as Count Something-or-other, and seemed a very decent fellow. He could not talk a word of English. He then called out his subalterns and formally introduced them with much clicking of heels and saluting. They were all very well turned out, while I was in a goatskin coat. One of the subalterns could talk a

107

few words of English. I said . . . 'My orders are to keep my men in the trenches and allow no armistice. Don't you think it is dangerous, all your men running about in the open like this? Someone may open fire.'

He called out an order, and all his men went back to their parapet, leaving me and the five German officers and a barrel of beer in the middle of No Man's Land.

. . . He said, 'You had better take the beer; we have lots.' So I called up two men to bring the barrel to our side. I did not like to take their beer without giving something in exchange, and I suddenly had a brainwave. We had lots of plum puddings, so I sent for one and formally presented it to him in exchange for the beer. He then called out 'Waiter', and a German private whipped out six glasses and two bottles of beer, and with much bowing and saluting we solemnly drank it, amid cheers from both sides. We then all formally saluted and returned to our lines. Our men had sing-songs, ditto the enemy.

So Stockwell reported cautiously to higher authority, while Richards recalled, more believably, but with less to lose, 'mucking in all day' with the Germans, and sharing their surpluses of tinned dinners. The men had

'Machonochie's and a decent portion of plum pudding. A tin of Machonochie's consisted of meat, potatoes, beans and other vegetables and could be eaten cold, but we generally used to fry them up in the tin on a fire.' The concoction—'meat and veg'—was as omnipresent as Spam would be to GIs in the next war. Except for captured stores, the Germans were about to enjoy their first sampling of what Tommies sang about by its initials:

Oh, a little bit of everything
Got in a tin one day,
And they packed it up and sealed it
In a most mysterious way;
And some Brass Hat came and tasted it,
And ' 'Pon me, Sam,' says he,
'We shall feed it to the soldiers
And we'll call it M and V.'

'Two barrels of beer were drunk,' Richards wrote, 'and the German officer was right: if it were possible for a man to have drunk the two barrels himself he would have bursted before he got drunk. French beer was rotten stuff.' The gift suds (actually Rhenish lager from a town north of Koblenz) seemed to the Welch on a par with German rations (too fatty) and tobacco (too strong).

Both sides preferred the rare harvest of fresh meat, secured from rear-area farms by stealth or from the creatures surviving in No Man's Land. Both found their way into the pots of enterprising soldiers. As Edward Hulse's men finished a chorus of 'Auld Lang Syne', one potential dish, a bewildered rabbit, popped out of the cabbages. Chasing after it, men on both sides slipped and slid on the frozen turf. After a hot two minutes,' Hulse wrote, 'we killed [it] in the open, a German and one of our fellows falling together upon the completely baffled hare. Shortly afterwards we saw four more hares, and killed one again; both were good heavy weight and had evidently been out between the two rows of cabbages for the last two months, and well fed . . . The enemy kept one and we kept the other.'

'We ate their Sauerkraut,' Charles Smith of the 6th Cheshires wrote in their battalion history about their positions near Bailleul, 'and they [ate] our chocolate, cakes, etc. We had killed a pig just behind our lines. There were quite a lot of creatures rambling about the lines, including an old sow with a litter and lots of cattle and poultry. We cooked the pig in No Man's Land, sharing it with the Boche.'

What attracted the barter-obsessed British more than food and drink were German uniform accessories, from buttons and belt buckles to the most desirable souvenir of all— the impractical and obsolescent *Pickelhaube*, about as useful as the tall black bearskin worn at Buckingham Palace at the changing of the guard. The spiked helmet, soon to be replaced by the fitted steel headgear familiar in two world wars, symbolized Prussian militarism and appeared in newspaper cartoons identifying *Junker* with enemy. A London Rifles entrepreneur, offering large quantities of appropriated bully beef and jam, acquired a prized *Pickelhaube,* which was nearly impossible to conceal or cart home. The day after Christmas he heard someone shouting for him from the German side. They met in No Man's Land. 'Yesterday,' his new friend appealed, 'I give my hat for the Bullybif. I have grand inspection tomorrow. You lend me and I bring it back after.' Somehow the deal was kept.

Next most prized in Christmas exchanges was the German uniform belt. Graham Williams of the London Rifles swapped his black metal shoulder insignia reading '5th City of London' for a German leather belt with brass buttons and a buckle embossed with *Gott mit uns,* and used it 'all through the war to keep up my trousers'. Some in his brigade thought—since Cockneys dropped the *h*—that the motto claimed divine intercession on the 'Hun' side. Warnings against swapping buttons and badges had little effect, for such portable prizes inevitably changed ownership, whether removed by the living or plucked from the dead.

Bruce Bairnsfather took a fancy to a German lieutenant's buttons, and despite language problems 'brought out my wire-clippers, and with a few deft snips, removed a couple of his buttons . . . I gave him two of mine in exchange'. Another bargain, reported in a letter to the *Daily Telegraph,* had an officer present a copy of *Punch* 'to a dingy Saxon in exchange for a small packet of excellent cigars and cigarettes'. It prompted *Punch*'s editor and resident satirist, Sir Owen Seaman, to publish (on 13 January, 1915) verses mockingly chastising the writer:

A scent of truce was in the air,
    And mutual compliments were paid—
A sausage here, a mince-pie there,
    In lieu of bomb and hand-grenade;
And foes forgot, that Christmastide,
    Their business was to kill the other side.
Then, greatly shocked, you rose and said,
    'This is not my idea of War;
On milk of human-kindness fed,
    Our men will lose their taste for gore;
All this unauthorized good-will
    Must be corrected by a bitter-pill.'

Although Seaman's bitter pill was identified, ironically, as his comic weekly, his humour was inadvertently subversive. The war was solving nothing.

Peaceable 'mucking about' was widespread,

112

more than Buffalo Bill or anyone else limited to a sector view could have imagined. In No Man's Land, enemies up and down the line gathered together for Christmas dinner— much of the menu from gift packages to improve the day. Although the circumstances were rarely the equal of the meal, some dinners were better than good and some venues were surprisingly fine. An officer who wrote to *The Times* shared, with his mixed party, 'pheasant and partridge and plum pudding, and *pâté de foie gras*' washed down with rum cut with hot water, 'eaten in a house which really as a house is wasting its time. The upper floor has simply gone.' Captain C. A. E. Chudleigh of the 2nd Leicesters saw through the loophole of his parapet soldiers 'moving freely about' on the enemy parapet opposite. He had no idea that some were his own men. When they drifted back from exchanging trophies and eating dinner, his sergeant-major reported an abnormal number of men 'missing'. Two of his reliable old soldiers finally returned, explaining that under a long, covered part of the enemy trench, a Christmas dinner had been laid out. The Germans had repeatedly urged them to stay, and when they declined, 'dragged them bodily into the trench by their legs'. The enforced dinner had been excellent, they boasted, far better than Maconochie's menu, and was interrupted only by an orderly—a waiter in Leicester before the war—ceremoniously presenting them with a bottle of French wine 'from the German officer to the English captain'. But the Tommies 'begged pardon' to Chudleigh, as they had not understood and had drunk it themselves.

A few hours later a message arrived with an unenforceable order from regimental headquarters: 'All fraternization with the enemy is to cease immediately. Any further action of this sort will be dealt with severely.' Chudleigh 'went into my funk hole, lit the stump of a candle and wrote a letter home from which these notes are taken'.

Fraternization came late to the British-officered Garhwals near Neuve-Chapelle who had been bemused on Christmas Eve by the lighted trees so reminiscent of Indian custom. For the Garhwals the sudden freeze was no improvement over the cold rain and mucilaginous mud. They oiled themselves under their uniforms to keep out the chill, and wound scarves and shawls over their greatcoats while baking their own bread with imported chapatti flour and cooking goat meat shipped from Corsica as alternative to beef and pork. They had no interest in Dickensian Christmas dinners or sentimental carols but were transfixed by the antics of Captain Walther Stennes's 3rd Westphalians, who tested the holiday frame of mind opposite by lifting their caps, on sticks, above the trenches to tempt a bullet. 'Of course we could not shoot them in cold blood,' said Captain E. R. P. Berryman, adjutant of the Garhwals' 2nd Battalion, 'tho' one or two shots were fired.'

Finally the Germans clustered atop their parapets and tempted the Garhwals with boxes of cigars and cigarettes. The troops mingled, and soon the cheering Germans were sitting on a Garhwals' parapet. One Westphalian told Colonel D. H. Drake-Brockman, commander of the 39th Garhwals, who was competent in German, that it was necessary to have *'Friede auf der Erde'*—at least at Christmas. Real peace, he thought, would come soon, as the Germans were winning on both fronts. 'The Russians are quite out of it.' He offered newspapers as corroboration. (In William Douglas-Home's play, *Christmas Truce*, Colonel Reid asks his counterpart, von Hassall, 'You speak English damned well. Have you been there?' *'Nein,'* says the Oberst confidently, 'I go next year. In the spring. When your army is beaten and we occupy your country.')

According to a 'trench yarn' in which officers from the opposing sides 'strolled about' between the lines chatting, an English subaltern identified only as 'Harry' and obviously a clubman, confessed, 'I would give a good deal for a bottle of the Boy now!'—a term for champagne popularized by Edward VII when Prince of Wales. 'My dear chap, nothing easier,' said the Bavarian. 'We've got quite a decent cellar at Headquarters on our side. Come and have a noggin in our Mess, won't you? Of course it's well behind our line, but I can promise you you'll be safe . . . You know we "play the game", as you English say.'

Regulations forbade it. Yet it was Christmas. They walked gamely through the supporting defences the English were not supposed to see, the German lieutenant apologizing for the 'nasty mess of the countryside . . . your gunners have made'. And the Englishman realized that he was being escorted to a farmhouse 'that he had personally reported to be blown up and made altogether uninhabitable'.

In the comfortable cellar, furnished from nearby ruined châteauxs, he sampled a Veuve Cliquot 1909, and noticed a copy of the *Daily Mail* only five days old. 'Not a bad spot for wartime, this, is it?' said the Bavarian. They raised their glasses, after which Harry confessed, 'Look here. You've put me in a damned awkward position by all this. You see, I was the observing officer when we strafed you, and I reported that the whole place had been blown to bits!'

'You're a nation of sportsmen,' insisted the lieutenant, 'and I am as certain as I am of anything that when you go back you'll have forgotten everything you saw here. Isn't that so? Have another glass of champagne?' They exchanged cards, and promised to meet after the war in both London and Munich, close to where there was some 'pretty good shooting'. Parting halfway between the lines with firm handshakes, they exchanged wishes for a good new year. 'Oh, by the by,' said the Bavarian as he turned back, 'on Thursday'—New Year's Eve—'we are relieved by the Prussians. Give 'em hell; we hate them!'

Harry's story is exceptional, but during the truce soldiers commonly spent time sampling the enemy's rations as well as their own. Gourmet fare, as always, was available only to the higher-ups, and—among lesser eminences—those with the best connections. Perhaps the most epicurean dinner was served in a cushy cellar in an otherwise ordinary château in Erquinghem, abandoned but for the domestics left behind. Lieutenant John Reith, transport officer of the 5th Scottish Rifles, occupied it while arranging the battalion's move into reserve near Armentières the next morning. But Reith, who 'did not propose to wage any war' on Christmas Day, ordered the three maids still upstairs to deck out tables in the safer cellar with the house's best crockery, cutlery and crystal. Then the nine men of the transport unit, ranging down to private, enjoyed a candle-lit dinner complete to the family's champagne.

Just after midnight, festivities were

interrupted by a messenger bringing Reith urgent news, but the runner was awed into speechlessness by the vision of linen and silver. The managerial ingenuity of transport officers was already legendary, but he was a private from the line. War was not like that. 'Good evening.' said the future founding director of the BBC imperturbably, although it was already morning of the next day. 'Come in and sit down.' After a glass of champagne the messenger hardly remembered that he bore any tidings.

The superior menu at British Headquarters at St Omer was shared by Field Marshal Sir John French with his ranking generals, Haig and Smith-Dorrien. At lunch French also offered each a Christmas gift. He was splitting the expanding British Expeditionary Force into two armies, effective the next day. Haig would command the First Army, Smith-Dorrien the Second Army. Earlier that morning, French had motored over to Marshal Foch at Cassel to advise him of the appointments and to present, for Christmas, a cigarette case and English cigars.

At German headquarters in the Belgian resort town of Spa, so famous for its salubrious waters that it gave a noun to the language, Kaiser Wilhelm, resplendent in an oversized field marshal's uniform with unearned medals and gaudy orders and decorations that meant little more than Christmas tree ornaments, celebrated the holiday among the aristocrats in his army. His Court circular would boast that His Imperial Majesty had shared the festive day with his troops in occupied Belgium, which somehow suggested the front. Rather, the front came to him. Escorted to a church on the market square by the First and Third Guards Regiments and the Guards Artillery, and their bands, the Kaiser, accompanied by his son Prince Eitel, took salutes and the tipping of flags.

The few men in the ranks were fortunate officers' aides; the officers themselves were splendidly attired in dress uniforms with red-striped headquarters trousers and no more traces of Flanders mud than British officerdom with their scarlet GHQ lapel tabs displayed at St Omer. The commandeered Grand Hotel Britannique at Spa, however, was no mere country château occupied by high brass. Its ballrooms were arrayed with gift tables, each topped by a small *Tannenbaum* shimmering with candlelight. The walls and ceilings were hung with fir branches. Gathered around rows of tables laden with festive delicacies and drinks were 960 invited guests. Each officer and orderly sampled spice cakes, apples, nuts and more meaty fare; there were no flaming plum puddings.

At one side of the main ballroom where tall Christmas trees stood on each side of an improvised altar draped with heavy hangings, an officer led the assemblage in '*O, du selige; o, du fröhliche Weihnachtszeit*', and Kaiser Wilhelm, his withered left arm tucked behind his back in a foreshortened uniform sleeve, strode forward to greet his '*Kameraden*'. A Lutheran pastor followed with a brief sermon, and '*Stille Nacht, heilige Nacht*' was sung with much less feeling than in the trenches. His Imperial Majesty offered the homily, which included an interpretation of the war which, however given to fantasy, the Kaiser could not have believed even as he spoke the words. 'God permitted the enemy to compel us to celebrate this festival here,' he declared. 'We are attacked. We defend ourselves. God grant that out of the hard struggle a rich victory may arise for us and our country. We stand on hostile soil, the points of our swords turned to the enemy, our hearts turned to God.' Closing, he quoted Otto von Bismarck: 'To the dust with all enemies of Germany! Amen.' And off went the favoured few to their Christmas dinners.

For less comfortable troops on the line, the surprising Christmas was, at the least, a reprieve from death, and an opportunity to drown their mixed emotions in more plebeian drink. Drunkenness raised extraordinarily few discipline problems on the line; yet almost everywhere alcoholic refreshment was offered by one enemy or another, usually the better-provisioned Germans, who had liberated

Belgian and French stores and brought their own beer and *Schnaps*. On Christmas night, Charles Toussaint of the 74th Regiment noted, a *poilu* 'perhaps under the influence of the nocturnal libations, let himself be carried away by the Germans . . . They brought him back, dead drunk, as far as the limit of our barbed wire, where we recovered him.'

In the valley of the Aisne, to the south, French and German troops had been less friendly, and when the Germans left their trenches on Christmas morning shouting 'Two days' truce!' the French had shot at them. But one German unit commanded by a Bavarian prince had behaved with great gallantry against the *poilu* in the days preceding Christmas, and a French captain who happened to be a musician felt that he owed the enemy opposite a composition of his own to mark the holiday. He organized those of his company who carried musical instruments with them into an impromptu orchestra of trumpets, accordions and a lone violin, and drafted an elaborate programme announcing a concert at 5:00 P.M. The invitation was tied to a rock and thrown across into the German trenches. On the hour, to a fanfare of trumpets, the captain climbed atop his parapet armed only with a baton. The concert went on, complete to the closing *Marseillaise,* after which his Bavarian counterpart stepped forward from his trenches and saluted, while troops on both sides cheered.

One-sided friendliness sometimes led to unfriendly fire, but most units, even when puzzled by the sudden shift from belligerence to *Bruderschaft,* accepted it as a gift. 'What were our men to do? Shoot?' asked Count Edward Gleichen, a brigadier with Boer War experience whose father was a cousin of Queen Victoria—a Hohenlohe-Langeburg who had emigrated to England and risen to Royal Navy admiral. 'You could not shoot unarmed men. Let them come? You could not let them come into your trenches; so the only thing feasible at the moment was done—and some of our men met them half-way . . . We got into trouble for doing it. But after all, it is difficult to see what we could otherwise have done, unless we shot the first unarmed man who showed himself—*pour encourager les autres.*' From Neuve Église, where Gleichen spent Christmas, he condoned the exchanges of 'seasonable remarks' and souvenirs, claiming in brass-hat defence, 'Meanwhile our officers got excellent close views of the German trenches, and we profited accordingly.'

On the Allied side of the line, a wry ballad later recalled the exchanges of food but not of drink, describing how men happily if temporarily forgot 'we'd gone there for a war':

Living it up, living it up,

The best way that we can,
On bully beef and biscuits
And pots of Tickler's jam,
Machonochie's and Bovril—
It really will be grand.
Doing the military two-step
With the Boche in No Man's Land.

CHAPTER FIVE

FOOTBALL

A Chinese fourth century B.C. military text mentions a primitive form of football. Roman soldiers played what they called *harpastum* and spread their version of soccer through the Continent and into Britain. Although Edward II tried to ban football in 1314, centuries later Shakespeare refers to it gaily in his *Comedy of Errors,* and in his *Henry V,* King Harry charges his men to advance with 'The game's afoot!' No soldier would have misunderstood. In Britain, which developed a love affair with soccer in the early nineteenth century, it became 'almost the manual workers' religion'. Captain J. L. Jack, later a general, observed, 'However tired the rascals may be for parades, they always have enough energy for football.' In the trenches there were no parades. General Haig was thinking of later, less desperate, times when he remarked that no troops travelled without a football. Balls were in short supply at Christmas 1914, although—perhaps after the events of that December—by the winter of 1917 every platoon was issued a regulation ball.

Football was not on Phillip Maddison's mind as he pedalled back toward the shattered château where he intended to conceal his ancient bicycle. As he bumped over the ruts a Tommy shouted to him that 'everyone' was out of the trenches and milling in No Man's Land—'talking to the Alleymans', he explained excitedly. 'There's bloody hundreds on'm, Jock!' Maddison cycled past the ruined house until he came to 'what on first sight looked like a crowd on a football field during the interval of a match'. Although the sporting image came to him, he had seen no play in the service, and very likely had also missed seeing a two months' old issue of *Punch* with a cartoon titled 'The Greater Game'. There old Mr Punch tells a sturdy Professional Association player, ball in hand and a boisterous throng in the stands behind him, 'No doubt you can make money in this field, my friend, but there's only one field to-day where you can get honour.' Maddison was on it, but honour had nothing to do with his being there.

Although the sandbag barricade blocking the remains of a road remained in place at the front line wire, what he saw beyond seemed like a dream, as did his standing erect in No Man's Land in daylight. Beyond was a breastwork—the enemy parapets. Leaning his bicycle against the forward British barricade, he walked on 'and found himself face to face with living Germans, men in grey uniforms and leather knee-boots'. Some were chatting in halting English to soldiers in British garb. One Fritz was carefully writing his name and address on a scrap of paper. They were arranging to write after the war.

The Germans appeared less fearsome close up than Maddison expected. Many were bareheaded in the pale sunlight. Others wore grey forage hats—*Feldmutzen*—with red bands, each with two metal buttons. 'They are Saxons,' a friendly, bearded German told him. 'They watched some of the London 'Ighlanders—your lot, mate—putting up a [wire] fence last night, but they wouldn't fire . . . even if they was ordered to. Or if they was forced to, like, they said they'd fire 'igh.'

Maddison said that he watched the other side put up a Christmas tree the night before. Looking up, he tried unobtrusively to plot the disposition of their trenches, seemingly in three rows at intervals of at least two hundred yards. Then he turned to someone he recognized from a 'new draft' recently arrived, and remarked about how many troops the enemy seemed to have, compared to their own

125

'mere scratches'. Lieutenant Glass identified some tough-looking Germans 'with green lanyards and tassels on their shoulders' as wearing sniper's cords. 'They're Prussians.' Maddison observed that they 'did not look at all friendly'. They had large round heads, and stood apart. The Saxons and Prussians didn't like each other, said Glass.

One Saxon was standing by himself, contentedly puffing on a large meerschaum pipe that had the look of an official Christmas gift. Maddison noticed that the glazed bowl displayed the face and high-peaked cap of 'Little Willie'—the *Kronprinz*. When Fritz realized he was being stared at, he plucked the pipe from his mouth and waved it, explaining, approvingly, *'Kronprinz! Prächtig[er] Kerl!!'*

'Cheer-ho!' Maddison said, to be polite, and another Saxon volunteered, *'Prächtig[er] Kerl* means good chap, or decent fellow. What you would call proper toff in Piccadilly. The *Kronprinz* Wilhelm gave us all a pipe. Jolly fine Christmas box, eh?'

'Jolly fine,' said Maddison, unrecognized in his rough dress as an officer. 'You speak very good English.' The Saxon explained that he had been a waiter at the Regent Palace Hotel for two years. Maddison confessed that he knew nothing of Germany or the language, but had cousins in Bavaria.

Shortly afterwards another companion, Lieutenant Church, amused by the fealty to the fatuous Crown Prince, observed, 'Fancy thinking that [positively] about Little Willie! But I suppose they don't realize what an absolute ass the fellow really is!'

They were 'driven on' by their officers, suggested another Scot, but Church dismissed that as 'rot', contending that both sides were fed propaganda 'lies' printed in their newspapers. Another listener argued that the Germans were smarter than the rhetoric they repeated. In fact, he said, the Germans were capable of intercepting front-line Morse code signals, his evidence being that after Sergeant Harvey-Lowther's field commission came through, a signboard was hoisted in the trenches opposite lettered, 'CONGRAT-ULATIONS, MR HARVEY-LOWTHER'. He described other and more imaginary intelligence coups, including the hoary one of the German co-opting of a Flemish farmer to plough furrows in the shape of arrows directing fire at English artillery positions.

They were well prepared for the war, agreed a Canadian Black Watch soldier, and Maddison conceded that. 'Well, I know one thing. Their trouser buttons are duplicated, in case of one coming off. They even thought of that detail!'

'Not like us!' they concurred, pointing to being sent out from England in spats and shoes, and with 'the wrong rifles'.

After bartering successfully for a trophy

Kronprinz meerschaum, Maddison slipped through from the swarming troops. Reclaiming his half-hidden bike, he pedalled off, looking for the London Rifles. The villages of Messines and Wytschaete—'White Sheet' to the English—were fairly close. He asked a German who was looking at his watch for the time and subtracted an hour. 'You are an hour before us,' Maddison explained.

'Yes,' agreed the German. 'That is our proper place in the sun.' So the Kaiser had boasted about Germany's imperial dreams for colonial parity with Britain.

The central British metaphor, as the Bavarian lieutenant had employed it in escorting 'Harry' into his lines, remained 'playing the game'. Patriotic verses by imperialist poet Sir Henry Newbolt which closed with the rallying cry 'Play up! Play up! And play the game!' had been much recited by schoolboys. The game he had in mind was gentlemanly cricket, but in 1914 a recruiting poster showing distant soldiers firing was superimposed on the exhortation, 'Play the greater game and join the football battalion'. With that working-class call to arms fresh, Maddison should not have been surprised when, cycling on through the lines, he saw something that looked like a soccer ball kicked into the air, and several soldiers running after it. A match had been proposed, he learned, to be played in a field behind the German trenches.

Whether a game of 'footer' actually occurred *inside* German lines is unproven, but references to football along the Flanders front are numerous. Unit histories are replete with reports of matches within their own lines, others played with the Germans themselves in No Man's Land. One Highlander reported talking during the truce with a footballer from Leipzig who boasted of having been in Britain the year before with his home eleven, when they 'beat Glasgow Celtic'. There is no record of the match, but he may have inflated their prowess. (Another German claimed to have played for Nottingham.) The Leipziger also proposed a two-hour 'interval' the next day, Boxing Day in Britain, for competition. 'This, however, was prevented by our superiors at HQ.' Another Saxon, who had been a waiter at a restaurant in the Fulham Road, 'was anxious to know,' Lieutenant H. Barrington-Brown recalled, 'how Fulham was doing in the F[ootball] A[ssociation] Cup.' Lance Corporal Hines of the Westminsters reported in the *Chester Chronicle* of 9 January 1915, that a German he encountered on the line identified himself, 'Good morning, sir; I [used to] live at Alexander-road, Hornsey. And I would see Woolwich Arsenal play Tottenham to-morrow.'

On Christmas Day itself at many locations along the front something resembling football

129

occurred. Private William Tapp of the Warwickshires wrote at Christmas from just above Ploegsteert Wood, 'We are trying to arrange a football match with them'—the Saxons—'for tomorrow, Boxing Day.' Harassing British artillery fire, he claimed later, prevented it. There were other plans for competition, right up to New Year's Day, once the clearance of corpses from No Man's Land had exposed potential fields for play. However dotted by half-hidden turnips and cabbages, the spaces between the lines were at least as wide as a conventional soccer pitch. A London Rifles officer whose letter appeared in *The Times* on 1 January reported that 'on Christmas Day a football match was played between them and us in front of the trench'. Perhaps because it was more appropriate later to deny it, the brigade's official history would claim that no match happened, 'because it would have been most unwise to allow the Germans to know how weakly the British trenches were held'. [The official denial, despite testimony from participants, that a Rifles Brigade match occurred with the Germans is in A.S. Bates, C. Harrison Jones, H.G., Wilkinson et al., *The History of the London Rifle Brigade, 1859–1919* (London, 1921).]

Dug in on the north flank of the Rifles, fronting Ploegsteert Wood, Frank and Maurice Wray saw also that 'a Battalion of the 10th

Brigade on our left arranged a football match against a German team, one of their number having contacted in the opposing unit a fellow member of his local football club in Liverpool.' The next day another Rifles officer—the very one who had deplored fraternization on Christmas Eve—described a scrimmage in which the Germans, while not participants, were in the appreciative audience. 'It's really an extraordinary state of affairs. We had an inter-platoon game of football in the afternoon; a cap-comforter stuffed with straw did for the ball, much to the Saxons' amusement.' W. V. Mathews of the Queen's Westminsters recalled, 'We got out of our trenches in the morning and played football, and then went out in front [of the line] and walked over to meet [the Germans]. We then shook hands and exchanged souvenirs . . . They could talk English, and it gave me an opportunity of exercising my little German.' G. A. Farmer of the Westminsters 'found our men playing football at the back of the[ir] trench, and the enemy walking about on the top of their trench [and watching]. It was hard to think we were at war with one another.' But they could not induce the Germans in their sector to join in, although the Tommies moved their pitch forward. As another Westminsters rifleman wrote, 'We had a football out in front of the trenches and asked the Germans to send a team to play us but either they considered the ground too hard, as it had been freezing all night and was a ploughed field, or their officers put the bar up.'

The Argylls and Sutherlanders did have 'a football match' with the Germans 'between the lines and the trenches', according to a sergeant from Longside, and Lieutenant Albert Winn of the Royal Field Artillery wrote, 'Around the Ypres area, on Christmas morning . . . we (the British, French and Germans) played football in No Man's Land. The . . . game ended in a draw.' He identified the opposition as 'Prussians & Hanovers' and the sporting cease-fire as lasting only that day. 'By midnight, the shells opened up and we were at it again.'

On 1 January, 1915, *The Times* published a letter from a major in the Medical Corps reporting that in his sector, after the Saxons sang 'God Save the King' to 'our people', one of his men 'was given a bottle of wine to drink the King's health', following which his regiment 'actually had a football match with the Saxons, who beat them 3–2!!!' The English account is supported by the official war history of the 133rd Saxon Regiment, which described the 'droll scene' of *'Tommy and Fritz'* first chasing down hares fleeing from under the cabbages, then kicking about a football furnished by a Scot. 'This developed into a regulation football match with caps [In a football scene in Bill Bryden' s 'epic' popular theatre piece, *The Big Picnic* (1994), the

Germans put their helmets down as goalposts, the Scots their 'Balmorals'—round, flat woollen caps.] casually laid out as goals. The frozen ground was no great matter. Then we organized each side into teams, lining up in motley rows, the football in the centre.' The result: *'Das Spiel endete 3:2 für Fritz!'* A Saxon ('one of us') took a photograph, but it is not reproduced in the official history. (Even the French of the 104th and 106th Infantry reported kilted Scots—very likely Argyll and Sutherland Highlanders—bringing a football and exchanging bottles of rum for 'schnapps'.) Hugo Klemm of the 133rd remembered, 'Everywhere you looked, the occupants of the trenches stood about talking to each other and even playing football.' In Hamburg in 1969 *Oberstleutnant* Johannes Niemann recalled the scene and the score, adding with delight, At this soccer match our privates soon discovered that the Scots wore no underpants under their kilts so that their behinds became clearly visible any time their skirts moved in the wind. We had a lot of fun with that, and in the beginning we just couldn't believe it . . . I myself got a private lesson one later time when I was seriously wounded and lay on the floor of a British ambulance, with four lightly wounded Scotsmen sitting on a supporting bar right over me.'

Sergeant Bob Lovell of the 3rd London Rifles played at footer, and although his side lost, the fact that the match had happened at all left him in awe. 'Even as I write,' he noted at dusk, 'I can scarcely credit what I have seen and done. It has indeed been a wonderful day.' Kurt Zehmisch of the 134th Saxons reported in his diary a rare authentic ball: 'Eventually the English brought a soccer ball from their trenches, and pretty soon a lively game ensued. How marvellously wonderful, yet how strange it was. The English officers felt the same way about it. Thus Christmas, the celebration of Love, managed to bring mortal enemies together as our friends for a time . . . I told them we didn't want to shoot on the Second Day of Christmas either. They agreed. Towards evening the [English] officers inquired as to whether a big soccer match could take place between our two positions tomorrow. However we could not make any promise . . . since, as we told them, there would be another captain here tomorrow.' They were to rotate with the 1st Company. The Saxons parted for their trenches with hearty handshakes.

Lieutenant Charles Brewer of the 2nd Bedfordshires wrote home, 'Higher up in the line—you would scarcely believe it—they are playing a football match.' And a history of the Lancashire Fusiliers records that its 'A' Company played a Christmas game against the enemy just north of Le Touquet, using a ration tin for a ball, and lost 3–2. The recorded scores echo others, but the specifics differ. Corporal William Hunt of the Nottingham and Derby Regiment (Sherwood Foresters), whose civilian working time had been spent under ground at the Huckleton Colliery, wrote of Christmas afternoon football play that 'not . . . the slightest notice' was taken of shell bursts 'when a football match is on the go'. Artillery rounds were as difficult to anticipate as sniper fire, and eager participants took their chances.

Corporal George Ashurst, somewhere on the line with the Lancashires, mentioned that 'some of our boys tied up a sandbag and used it as a football' that afternoon—not the same game although the same brigade. An officer whose letter appeared in the *Morning Post* described 'a game of football going on' as well as 'bicycle races on bikes without tyres found in the ruins of the houses'. Lieutenant R. St. John Richards of the Welch Fusiliers wrote home to Llangyniew Rectory, 'I must say that to a casual onlooker it would have appeared that we were friends, not foes. Some of the more sportive even got out a football, and we had a sort of friendly match. They were a Saxon corps.'

Diaries, letters and recollections on both sides describe makeshift footballs; few deplore the grossly untidy condition of the pitch. An infantry colonel wrote to his wife on Christmas Day (the letter appeared in the *Daily Telegraph* on 2 January, 1915) that the regimental

135

physician had 'boldly walked down the road' to the German trenches and found the Saxons 'very full of the football idea of mine on New Year's Day . . . I would turn out a team and play them among the shell-holes, and they were quite keen'. Private Alexander Runcie of the 6th Gordon Highlanders scoffed at the likelihood of a playable surface, lamenting that No Man's Land was 'impossible' because of 'the shellholes, ditch[es], barbed wire, and churned-up condition of this part of the ground'. Yet Private Geoff Gilbert wrote, forty-nine years later, about the Kensingtons to the north of Neuve-Chapelle, 'Soon there were dozens of us fraternizing even to the extent of kicking a made-up football about in No Man's Land.' Forty years later, Private Ernie Williams, once a Territorial in the 6th Cheshires, then east of Wulverghem, above the River Douve, recalled a match which another veteran of the Cheshires, Sergeant-Major Frank Nadin, had described (on 9 January, 1915 in the *Cheshire Post)* as 'a rare old jollification' which included the Germans. Captain Thomas ('Laurie') Frost of the 1st Cheshires wrote home to his father about 'a football match against the Germans' as early as 31 December, adding five pages on visits to German trenches and swapping plum puddings for sausages. 'It seems extraordinary,' he continued, 'that a desperate fight was going on during this about 800 yards to our left between the French and the Germans.' The Christmas idyll was an imperfect one, and it was remarkable indeed that fraternization and firing could go on within sight and sound of each other.

According to Ernie Williams of the Cheshires,

> The ball appeared from somewhere, I don't know where, but it came from their side . . . They made up some goals and one fellow went in [to score a] goal and then it was just a general kickabout. I should think there were about a couple of hundred taking part. I had a go at the ball. I was pretty good then, at 19. Everybody seemed to be enjoying themselves. There was no sort of ill-will between us . . . There was no referee, and no score, no tally at all. It was simply a mêlée—nothing like the soccer you see on television. The boots we wore were a menace—those great big boots we had on—and in those days the balls were made of leather and they soon got very soggy.

Robert Graves had been in his school Officers Training Corps at Charterhouse until his commissioning at nineteen, after a few weeks' training. He was posted as a replacement to the battered Royal Welch Fusiliers only in the spring of 1915, but heard enough then about what had happened at Christmas to recall the events imaginatively in his 'Christmas Truce', a story he did not publish until December 1962. In a boy's overheard conversation during a weekly 'Saturday night booze' between 'Grandfather' (or 'Fiddler') and his one-legged visitor also from the 'North Wessex Regiment' (the Welchs), one-time Private 'Dodger' Green, the familiar details emerge. On Christmas Eve the Saxon parapets opposite had lit up, and a Fritz with a megaphone shouted, 'Merry Christmas, Wessex!' Once the trenches still 'knee-deep in water' emptied of men, the Germans between the lines identified themselves as 'Saxons, same as us, from a town called Hully—' Halle.

The next day, Green remembers, Captain Pomeroy of the Wessex and Lieutenant Coburg of the Saxons arranged a match:

No Man's Land had seemed ten miles across when we were crawling out on a night patrol; but now we found it no wider than the width of two football pitches. We provided the football, and set up stretchers as goal posts; and the Rev. Jolly, our Padre, acted as ref. They beat us 3–2, but the Padre had shown too much Christian charity—their outside-left shot the deciding goal, but he was miles offside and admitted it as soon as

138

the whistle went. And we spectators were spread nearly two deep along the touch-lines with loaded rifles slung on our shoulders.

The provocative 'loaded rifles' was one of Graves's fictional touches, to hint at how a controversial decision might have been protested, but he described a peaceable competition, the distractions of mess call in their separate trenches, and the chasing after a hare spotted 'loping down the line' and pursued by both sides. 'There ain't no such thing as harriers in Germany,' says Dodger; 'they always use shot-guns on hares. But they weren't allowed to shoot this one, not with the truce.'

The football accounts, even in the official histories, suggest such delight among the enemies that their combat involved a ball or its equivalent rather than weapons (the only occasion in what would be fifty-two months of carnage) that neither side protested penalties which in peacetime play might have raised loud protests. Only in a television series in 1989 is there a recollection—an imaginative one—of a referee's ruling which remains a bone in the throat. In a *Blackadder* episode set on the Western Front in 1917, Captain Sir Edmund Blackadder, who claims to have joined the army when it was little more than a travel agency for gentlemen, recalls the

Debt of Honour Register

Name
Rank **Regiment**
Date of Death

BLACKADDER, A T
  Private   Royal Scots
28th Mar 1918

BLACKADDER, C
  Serjeant   London Regiment
15th Sep 1916

BLACKADDER, D A
  Private   London Regiment
26th May 1915

BLACKADDER, G B R
  Corporal   Highland Light Infantry
25th September 1915

BLACKADDER, J
  Private   Royal Scots
23rd Mar 1916

BLACKADDER, T
  Rifleman   Royal Irish Rifles
24th Mar 1917

The Commonwealth War Graves Commission lists six men with the surname Blackadder who died in the First World War.

Christmas kickabout. Still in Flanders, only twenty yards from the enemy, he reminds the stuffy Lieutenant George Colthurst St. Barleigh and their incompetent cook Private Baldrick of the pivotal accomplishment of his service career.

'We made out all right just before Christmas 1914,' Baldrick agrees.

'Yes, that's right,' says St. Barleigh. 'I'd just arrived and we had that wonderful Christmas truce. You remember, sir? You could hear "Silent Night" drifting across the clear, cold air of No Man's Land. Then they came—the Germans—emerging out of the freezing night mist, calling to us. And we clambered over the top to meet them.'

'Both sides,' says Blackadder ruefully, 'managed to advance more in one Christmas piss-up than they managed in the next two-and-a-half years of war.'

'Remember the football match?' Baldrick asks.

'Remember it?' contends Blackadder. 'How could I forget it? I was *never* off-side. I could not believe it!' Early the next morning they go over the top, and the screen fades to a field of Flanders poppies. (The Commonwealth War Graves Commission lists six dead surnamed Blackadder.)

In William Douglas Home's play *A Christmas Truce,* first produced the same year, neither side has a football. A British private,

John Smith, stuffs his woolly hat with mud and straw and ties it up, after which play against the Germans begins offstage. Over echoed cheers and catcalls, officers from both sides talk about 'pushing their luck' in stretching out the truce. The vigorously contested match furnishes a metaphor for the war, and Adam Brunkner, the German lieutenant, concedes the impossibility of the conflict ending as might a game, with no consequences— 'Because the Kaiser and the generals and politicians in my country order us that we fight.'

'So do ours,' agrees Andrew Wilson.

'Then what can we do?'

'The answer's "nothing". But if we do nothing . . . like we're doing now, and go on doing it, there'll be nothing they can do but send us home.'

'Or shoot us.'

'What, a million or two of you—or more— don't be daft. They wouldn't dare. Nor would our big-wigs either. That's what ought to happen.'

As the game continues offstage, Colonel Reid, Wilson's commander, stops by to watch, and warns that their own general wants the truce—not the war—to end, but is unlikely to be heavy-handed about it. 'And I'll tell you why. Because the top brass and the government know damned well that the public at home wouldn't stand for it, if people were court-martialled.' Not only was the public a lot of 'sentimental buggers' about Christmas, he realizes: 'I'd say that half the British Army has already written home or to the newspapers about it. You have, I'll bet.'

'I did mention it, sir,' Wilson confesses, 'in a letter to my father.'

Two chaplains emerge from the direction of the German trenches. 'They played extra time,' reports Major Spearpoint.

'Who won?'

'Their lot, sir. Three [to] one.'

Although Christmas 1914 is a phenomenon enriched by recollections of football, some of the details are too quirky to accept readily. One alleged post-football encounter is simply too surreal to have happened. According to Guardsman Harold Bryan of the Argyll and Sutherlanders, the Germans opposite offered beer and cigars for bully beef and biscuits while a cyclist pedalled to the British rear to find a football. 'Then we arranged a Boxing Contest. This was great fun in which I took no part, not wishing to be knocked about by a big Prussian Guard. The best match was between one of our men measured 6' 5½ in[che]s & a huge Prussian Guard of about the same height. These two hammered each other & would not give in until stopped by us owing to their faces being smashed up so badly.' Yet it was not over. The battered Scot 'suggested that each should be given a rifle & only one bullet, stand

143

or lay at 1 hundred yards from each other and on the word being given[,] fire. But this we would not allow seeing that we had called a truce for the day.' The abortive contest between champions suggests the medieval tournament and joust gone absurd. Yet Private J. Goggin of Stratford wrote home that 'a German called over to our trenches that he was willing to fight single-handed any man we cared to send, except an Irishman. His challenge was accepted by a Gordon Highlander, and the two met in front of the trenches for a good set-to with the bayonet. The German was killed after a hard fight.'

At the least, the Argylls had a kickabout. The laconic account of the sergeant from Longside confirming that there was a contest had appeared in the *Glasgow News* on 2 January. According to Bryan, the wan afternoon sun was setting, but from 'M & V' tins they concocted, between the lines, 'a huge Bully stew', consumed around large fires which furnished, the more optimistic thought, sufficient light for a game. After dinner, on the return of the cyclist with a ball, 'we played them a match[,] winning easily by 4–1. This ended the day.'

A subaltern writing sardonically to the *Liverpool Daily Post* reported that his unit agreed to play the Westphalians opposite, but it was not easy to do. 'The ground is all in root crops and all cut up in ditches, and moreover, we had not got a football. This rather recalls the story of the German burgomaster who, summoned to explain to his irate Grand Ducal Sovereign why his arrival at the little town had not been signalled by the ringing of joy bells, said first that the keys to the church could not be found; secondly, that the bellringers were all dead; and "Finally, your Majesty, there are no bells here".'

Some attempts at football were frustrating, and very likely other unreported games were played. It soon became risky to chance a footer, or to report it. A letter published in the *South Wales Echo* quotes an unnamed—but probably Welch Fusiliers—infantry battalion commander, 'I said if they would have an armistice on New Year's Day we would play them at football between the lines. In the afternoon at 3pm our doctor thought he would go and see the Germans, so we boldly walked down the road to the trenches and talked to them. They were very full of the football idea of mine . . . I said if they would like another armistice then I would turn out a team and play them among the shell holes, and they were quite keen. Happily, there won't be any obstacles like dead Germans lying about unless they try another attack before then. I wonder if it will come off?' Apparently it did not. Yet well below Armentières, near Loos, William Dawkins of the East Kents recalled many years later, 'the Germans came out of their protective holes, fetched a football, and invited our boys out for a little game. Our boys joined them and together they quickly had great fun, till they (I believe we were responsible) had to return to their posts. I cannot guarantee it, but it was told to me that our lieutenant colonel threatened our soldiers with machine guns. Had just one of these Big Mouths gathered together ten thousand footballs, what a happy solution that would have been, without bloodshed.'

Although the allegation of machine guns strains credibility, there were situations in which command hostility ended, or prevented, play. Lieutenant C. E. M. Richards of the 1st Lancashires, a career officer later a general, was exasperated by the fraternization and longed for some 'good old sniping . . . just to make sure the war was on'. Then on Christmas night he was ordered by battalion headquarters 'to make a football pitch in No Man's Land, by filling in the shell-holes . . . and to challenge the enemy to a football match.' Richards was 'furious and took no action at all'. There would be no football in his sector. Private Mullard of the Rifle Brigade wrote to his parents that his unit 'agreed to play a football match . . . on Christmas Day, and we got a ball ready, but their colonel would not allow them to play, so we had a game on our own'. Still, the Germans joined with the British, drank their tea and cocoa, and 'entertained each other with sing-songs' until darkness came, when they were ordered back. 'Just after midnight you could hear, away on the right, the plonk-plonk of the bullets as they hit the ground, and we knew the game had started again.'

Exasperated, too, was Oberstleutnant Gustav Riebensahm of the 2nd Westphalians, who had at first welcomed the surprising truce. A career officer, he had a mission that had been interrupted. The day after Christmas he noted in his diary, 'The English are said to have told the 53rd Regiment they are exceeding thankful for the truce because they simply had to play football again. The whole business is becoming ridiculous and must come to an end. I arranged with the 55th Regiment that the truce will end this evening.'

Worrying that the restart of the real game might trap him behind the German lines, Phillip Maddison wheeled his bicycle toward the German barricades. To his relief, the old machine with its hard, flat tyres and queer, high handlebars only amused a German sentry, and while the field-grey Fritzies were making for the field, and the football match from which Maddison had come, he pedalled on undisturbed into the village of Wytschaete toward the poplar-flanked road that appeared to go from Ypres to occupied but demolished Messines. Cottages that had somehow survived displayed fresh, white-painted German numbers on the doors, and a barn had the menacing words, painted boldly, 'GOTT STRAFE ENGLAND!' Outside a café was a bearded German smoking his Christmas meerschaum. Feeling 'white about the gills' with anxiety, Maddison decided to risk a salute, raising an arm from the handlebars, which made his cycle shudder nearly fatally. He also chanced his limited but suddenly essential German. *'Ja! Ja!'* he shouted, pointing to the white-bowled Christmas pipe, *'Kronprinz, prächtig[er] Kerl! auf Wiedersehen!'* Having exhausted his new vocabulary, he waved and wobbled on, hoping not to hear a shot fired in his direction.

He felt, still, as if he were in a dream, and realized that his impulsive adventure was stupid. Yet the exhilaration stirred by the strange Christmas kept him cycling into territory from which he had retreated earlier in the autumn. He recognized familiar landmarks, or the remnants of them, like the surviving wall of a red barn, and he stopped at a burial ground in which every German, whether identified or *unbekannt, 'ruht in Gott'*, but where each Englishman, according to the wooden crosses emplaced by their adversaries, only *'ruht'*. Yet the dead, there as everywhere, were on the same side.

Hoping to appear inconspicuous, Maddison kept pedalling while formulating for possible use, if stopped, an excuse for being behind enemy lines. The least awkward answer would be that he was looking for the football game. The wood he saw ahead looked familiarly like Plugstreet, and he hoped it was. Beyond it would be the London Rifles. From the angle of the sun he guessed it was English one o'clock—two on the German side. His front wheel now had two detached spokes pinging, and since he was headed slightly downhill, he decided to freewheel while he could. In his crude, sour-smelling goatskin coat, standard attire but in poor condition, and with his venerable and unmilitary bicycle, he hoped he might pass for a Flemish farmer, although no Belgian peasant wore kilts beneath.

In a clearing he saw grey-clad figures standing over something that on closer inspection turned out to be one of a battery of field guns. His mouth went dry. He was being stared at by Germans smoking new meerschaum pipes. There was no recourse but to the performance as before. In a voice thin and throaty from alarm he croaked, *'Bonjour, messieurs! Kronprinz prüchtig[er] Kerl! Hoch der Kaiser!'* He hoped that they wouldn't know what to make of him, but also that they wouldn't much care.

The road narrowed beyond and nearly disappeared in shell-holes half-hidden in ice. Maddison realized that he must be behind the German trenches and what appeared to be a sandbag barricade. He had to dismount and push his bicycle toward a forward parapet, frizzed with coils of mean-looking barbed wire. (German wire had more barbs per yard than the English equivalent.) Abandoning his wheels, his face now transparent with anxiety at what seemed to be a thousand enemy faces staring at him, he trudged fifty yards further toward a group of mudstained soldiers in a motley of khaki and grey. No Man's Land had never looked so hospitable.

His query seemed inane. 'Can you tell me the name of this place, please?'

'St Ives. 'Oo are yer?'

Maddison replied and thumbs jerked—'Down there.'

Through the fraternizing Fritzes and Tommies, and into the frozen turnip field, Maddison walked toward some cottages in the near distance. He asked again, and a soldier in khaki said, 'East Lancs, mate.' Maddison went on, past the Somersets and the Hampshires. 'I say, can you tell me where the London Rifles—?' he tried again, and he explained his foolhardy bicycle ride but found few believers. 'What, right behind their lines?' A knot of men clustered around him.

One of the Germans milling nearby was a tall officer who looked fixedly at him as Maddison was finishing his account. He worried about the concealed battery behind the wood, and his supposition was confirmed when the German said quietly, in English,

'May I have a word with you? Shall we walk this way, and see the *prie Dieu* at the Cross-Roads? We "Huns" have not yet succeeded in shooting it down, you will be able to observe, to the satisfaction of some of your newspapers.' The Germans, Maddison knew, read English papers acquired in trench raids. Ypres was only seventy miles from London, although as different as the Moon, and enterprising French newsboys pedalled forward hazardously with *The Times* and the *Daily Mail.* Even the post only took a couple of days to reach the front.

More remote in every way but miles was the Flanders world of relics and rites. Images of crucifixion rather than of Christmas—roadside Calvaries, each mounted on a three-step pyramid—were omnipresent wherever French or Belgian roads intersected, and Tommies referred to each breezily as Crucifix Corner. As they walked, the German pointed also to several new crosses of ration-box wood set up on newly dug graves. And he went on, 'May I count on the word of a . . . Highlander, that you will regard your recent visit behind our lines as, shall we say, never for a moment approximating to that of an agent?'

'An agent, sir?'

'A spy.'

'Oh, no, I wasn't for a moment spying, sir.' Maddison guessed that his identity as an officer was unperceived, although the kilts

151

under his long, open coat could give away everything else. He also realized, with a start, that they were being closely followed by a German soldier wearing a green shoulder cord, and he knew what that meant. His prepared football story would no longer do him any good.

'I am glad to hear it,' said the pink-faced, clean-shaven captain, 'otherwise you would be my prisoner, do you understand. We are still at war.'

'Yes, sir.'

'Then you give me your word?'

'Yes, sir.'

'Good. Now may I ask you some questions of purely personal interest to myself? How did your government supply you with so many Maxim guns . . . ?' Withering fire, he admitted, had forced the Germans to break off the battle and settle, at Ypres, for stalemate. Also, they were running out of reserves, and bringing in student replacements 'with one rifle among three'. Maddison ventured that the British had no Maxim guns there, and were using 'fifteen rounds rapid' rifles. And that while they had been short of reinforcements themselves, 'We've got a great many now!'

'Well—*auf Wiedersehen,* my English, or should I say Scottish friend?' the German closed, without offering his name or asking for Maddison's. 'This war will not last for ever. Perhaps we may meet again when it is over.

152

Until then, goodbye. I am happy to rely on your word.' He clicked his heels and bowed. With relief, Maddison came to attention, then bowed. As they moved toward their own lines, he mused about the 'extraordinary thing' his experience had been.

The adventure and its aftermath gave Williamson an opportunity to preach rapprochement. Both sides were misled by half-truths. Each side was more inefficient than the other assumed. Beneath the artificial hatred each respected the other. Victory, if it came at all, would be long delayed, costly and worthless. Perhaps a football match, after which both sides went home, might be better as a solution.

In Maddison's adventure, Williamson had improved upon his own experience in the 5th Battalion, London Rifles, although someone did indeed slip through the lines. Major A. G. Arbuthnot of the 24th Battery, Royal Field Artillery, one of his gunners remembered nearly fifty years later, 'put on a German uniform and had a good look around . . . He spotted what he wanted to find—a German machine-gun post which had given our infantry a deal of trouble.' Private Williamson—he was not yet an officer but would be commissioned after he was invalided home in January—also wanted to get behind enemy lines, 'but a German officer came up to me and asked, "What do you do?" "Admiring your beautiful

153

field fortifications," I told him. And he smiled and saluted and I went back and told my second lieutenant, who ordered me not to do it again.'

The appeal of a kickabout between enemies as the only way that war should be fought has an iconic quality which intensifies over the years. Looking at the links between *Bruderschaft* and competition, a book for children, *War Game* (1989), tells the story for a younger generation. Warmly written and illustrated by Michael Foreman, it focuses upon impromptu, untidy soccer play, as 'from somewhere, a football bounced across the frozen mud . . . immediately a vast, fast and furious football match was underway. Goals were marked by caps . . . Apart from that, it was wonderfully disorganized, part-football, part ice-skating, with unknown numbers on each team. No referee, no account of score. It was just terrific to be no longer an army of moles, but up and running on top of the ground that had threatened to entomb them for so long . . . The goalposts grew larger as greatcoats and tunics were discarded and the players warmed to the sport. Khaki and grey mixed together. Steam rose from their backs, and their faces were wreathed in smiles and clouds of breath in the clear frosty air.' And when the game comes to its 'exhausted end' and officers 'encourage' their troops back to the trenches, both sides hope for 'another

154

game' on another day.

A ghostly game of football in No Man's Land, accompanied by a voice-over of an actual reminiscence, was played in 1999–2000 at a simple diorama in the Football Association Premier League Hall of Fame in the former County Hall in London. Reliving the experience, one peered through slotted boards suggesting observation slits in the shelled ruin of a house in Flanders. Beyond was the starkness of the space between the trenches. Then the screen came to life. Projected onto it was an almost spectral fragment of black-and-white film reconstructing a shadowy kickabout between the troops on both sides. Then the scene faded, to be reawakened by the push buttons of viewers again and again. The exhibit has been dismantled but the memory lives.

CHAPTER SIX

HOW IT ENDED

In a striking foreshadowing of what was happening in Flanders, the American cartoon strip *Scoop the Cub Reporter* showed the flouting of the truce—although when drawn days earlier by 'Hop' for syndication the shooting hadn't stopped. A German soldier, protected by a *Pickelhaube,* ducks as enemy shells swish over his parapet. 'Here they come,' he complains, 'charging our trenches the day after Xmas. By golly—I just can't bear to fight so soon after Xmas.'

An idea surfaces. He impales his emptied Christmas stocking on a bayonet as a makeshift flag of truce and pokes it aloft as he hunkers down further. A charging English cavalryman, more medieval than modern, draws back on his reins. Turning toward the troops behind him he shouts, 'Halt!!! Who shoots a hole in yon Xmas sock gets a bullet in his block—Rightohbowoot face!' For the moment, the truce is preserved.

Although the truce seemed to end as it had begun—from the bottom up, with random acts of violence—the High Commands on both sides were also demanding renewed war, and by orders and threats they made it happen. Tradition on one side and discipline on the other made any other outcome impossible. The illegal truce was widespread but not effective everywhere. Ernst Jünger claimed to have been in the line on Christmas Eve singing carols while he and his men stood in the mud, their voices drowned out 'by the enemy machine-guns'. And on Christmas Day he lost a man in his 3rd Platoon 'by a flanking shot through the head'. After that, he contended, 'the English attempted a friendly overture and put up a *Weihnachtsbaum* on their parapet.

But our fellows were so embittered that they fired and knocked it over. In this miserable fashion we celebrated Christmas Day.'

The truce was never completely observed. Despite promises to do nothing belligerent, both sides brought up loads of wood and straw—'pioneer materials' in German parlance—to improve their dugouts, and additional barbed wire, undertaking tasks hazardous and sometimes impossible under fire. Much of the effort, however, was obviously defensive. 'I honestly believe,' a Guards officer said of enemy friendliness, 'that if I called on the Saxons for fatigue parties to help with our barbed wire, they would have come over and done so.' Accounts of that happening are many. In one, Lieutenant H. Barrington-Brown, later a colonel, when 'almost up to the knee in icy slush' observed 'a German officer sitting in a broken-down armchair evidently out of some ruined cottage, with his back to us on top of his parapet directing their digging operations. When low barbed wire was put down one of our men borrowed a maul from a Saxon to hammer stakes . . . The Saxons hated the Prussians & many Saxons said they & we ought to be on the same side.' Lieutenant Hulse explained realistically from his talks with the other side that the enemy would 'help us to put up our barbed wire' because they had enough of war and understood that 'all Belgium and a bit of

France' gave Germany 'a nice bit to bargain and barter with'.

Even among those who fraternized, tensions never fully eased. A Londoner in the 3rd Rifles had his hair cut by a Saxon who had been his barber in High Holborn. 'Blimey, Sarge,' a Tommy had remarked. 'This beats the lot. See that square 'ead on the right? I know the bloke.'

'Hey, Fritz! Fritzy!' he called. 'You cut my 'air for me, remember? In 'igh Holborn. Last June.'

Ach, yes, my friend,' said the Saxon. And now I give you short back-and-sides vunce more. Vait—I get my scissor.' Surrounded by friends and enemies, the rifleman sat on an ammunition box set among the shell craters while his hair was trimmed. And as the Saxon finished with a flourish of the traditional open razor, he joked, 'And maybe I should cut your throat today, yes? Save ammunition tomorrow.'

Even as intimacies grew in No Man's Land it was obvious that exasperation on the command level was eventually going to reverse the trend. The hostility to further games of footer had already shown that. It was difficult, however, for an Englishman to feel other than friendly toward men on the other side who seemed not only mirror images of themselves, but also spoke that way. 'Watcha cock,' one asked Graham Williams, 'how's London?'

158

'Good Lord,' said Williams, 'you speak like a Londoner.' ('Absolutely Cockney,' he thought.) And the German identified himself as 'a German Londoner' who had arrived as a child and went to school in England, but was recalled for national service before becoming a porter at Victoria Station. (After Sarajevo he was activated.) One Fritz shouted, 'Are you the Warwicks? Any Brummagem lads there?' He had a wife and five children in Birmingham. Near Armentières a German juggler who had performed in London and had a Cockney verve improvised a 'Cain and Abel' (rhyming slang for table) between the lines and went through what routines he could, to an eager audience of *Kameraden* and appreciative riflemen from the 3rd Londons. According to the battalion's war diary he 'drew a large crowd'. In the dumbfounding unexpectedness of the truce it would not have surprised anyone very greatly had the juggler turned out to be a modern Pied Piper and led a rapt throng of friends and enemies away from the front, 'determining the war['s end] for want of troops.'

No one embroidered the juggler's results quite that way, but in Robert Graves's version of the exhibition as told by 'Dodger Green', late on Christmas afternoon 'a funny-faced Fritz called Putzi' appeared in No Man's Land with a trestle table. 'He talked English like a Yank. Said he'd been in Ringling's Circus . . .

and put on a hell of a good gaff with conjuring tricks and juggling—had his face made up like a proper clown. Never heard such applause as we gave Herr Putzi!'

Unfortunately their belligerent brigadier makes one of his rare appearances at the front, 'sloshing up the communication trench, keeping his head well down'. Unable to warn the Germans in time, as everyone was so absorbed in watching Putzi Cohen, Captain Pomeroy shouts to Dodger, 'Private Green, run along the line and order the platoon commanders from me to fire three rounds rapid over the enemies' heads'. By the time that 'Old Horseflesh'—as they referred to the general at a distance—pops up, not a Fritz is visible. 'I was very glad,' the brigadier declares, 'to hear that Wessex fusillade, Pomeroy. Rumours have come in of fraternization elsewhere along the line. Bad show! Disgraceful! Can't interrupt the war for freedom just because of Christmas! Have you anything to report?'

Pomeroy keeps a straight face. 'Our sentries report that the enemy have put up a trestle table in No Man's Land, Sir. A bit of a puzzle, Sir. Seems to have a bowl of goldfish on it.' As Dodger Green recalls, 'Old Horseflesh removes his brass hat, takes his binoculars, and cautiously peeps over the parapet'—where a sea of humanity had been only minutes before. 'They are goldfish, by Gad!' he shouts. 'I wonder what new devilish trick the Hun will invent next. Send out a patrol tonight to investigate.' Pomeroy promises to do so.

His counterpart, Lieutenant Coburg, on his way to present a pair of leather gloves to the captain, Green recalls, has assumed that the shots must have come from the unrepentant Sherwood Foresters [The Sherwood Foresters actually did relieve the 2nd East Lancashires on Christmas Day.] on their flank, and wonders where everyone has gone. Across the line, still brandishing his binoculars, Old Horseflesh shoves a rifle into Green's hands. 'Take a steady aim,' he commands. Dodger aims well above Coburg's head, and the lieutenant dives into a handy shell hole. Catching on, the German machine gunners let loose a burst well above the opposite trenches. Hurrying to the rear, the brigadier catches his foot in a loop of telephone wire and falls face down into the mud. (The 6th Gordons reported such an order from a brigadier to a private, who fired sportingly high, was angrily commanded to 'shoot again', and this time fired close enough—but still deliberately awry—to cause an exposed German to 'dive headlong into his trench'.)

With Old Horseflesh gone, the Wessexers put up an ALL CLEAR board, and troops flood out again. Coburg emerges with the gloves for Pomeroy, who offers in return a Shetland scarf (an episode Graves apparently

161

drew from an actual exchange), warning that the General Staff may get wind of their lark. Coburg advises that the Prussians are to relieve his Saxons in two days. 'I suggest that we continue the truce until then, but with no more fraternization.' As a great favour, to butter up the brigadier, Pomeroy asks if he might 'capture' the bowl of goldfish. When Putzi Cohen protests, the captain offers a gold sovereign for the trophy, and unable to resist swapping goldfish for gold, Putzi relents. 'Please, for Chrissake,' he appeals, pocketing the coin, 'don't forget to change their water!'

'God knows,' Green muses, 'what Intelligence made of them goldfish when they were sent back to Corps H.Q . . . I expect someone decided the goldfish have some sort of use in trenches, like the canaries we take down to the coal pits.'

Parting from Lieutenant Coburg, Pomeroy predicts, 'From what I can see . . . there'll be stalemate on this front for a year or more. You can't crack our line, even with massed machine guns; and we can't crack yours. Mark my words: our Wessex and your Saxons will still be rotting here next Christmas—what's left of them.' Coburg, Dodger Green recalls, 'didn't agree, but he didn't argue'.

London Rifles sergeant Bob Lovell had seen the actual performance begin after his captain had sent a 'sack' of tea across the lines, and watched, too, the discontent of 'one grey-coated warrior' at the men from both sides who flocked amiably about the juggler. Tearing off his greatcoat and throwing it down in anger, he shouted to no one in particular, 'War? This is war? Well, I'm a . . .' And, Lovell claimed, the frustrated Fritz 'promptly burst into tears'. Unperturbed, a Saxon officer withdrew a *verboten* camera from his coat and took a photograph of a dozen men from both sides, posed with mistletoe and holly (from gift packages) in their caps and helmets, some soldiers in headgear exchanged—for the picture—with the enemy.

Some on both sides who opposed the truce found the recent deaths in the field of close comrades too bitter and too fresh to ignore; others worried about a relaxation in vigilance or in the will to kill. Toward the southern anchor of the British line, Major George Darrell Jeffreys of the 2nd Grenadier Guards had endured, with his men, a violent Christmas Eve and very unfriendly fire. The next morning 'a few Germans put their heads up and shouted "Merry Xmas". Our men, after yesterday, were not feeling that way, and shot at them. They at once replied and a sniping match went on all day.' Captain Billy Congreve of the 3rd Division, to the north at Kemmel (west of Wytschaete), needed no upscaled animosity to maintain his belligerence. 'We have issued strict orders to the men,' he noted in his diary, 'not on any account to allow a "truce", as we have heard they will try to. The Germans did try. They came over toward us singing. So we opened rapid fire on them, which is the only sort of truce they deserve.'

In areas where a wild or ricocheted round struck a peaceful fraternizer hundreds of yards off, the alarming possibility arose of a sudden restart to the war while thousands were still innocently in the open. Two 2nd Monmouthshires were shot while returning from friendly exchanges. Sergeant W. 'Blackwood' Jones, once a footballer in Pontypool, had led a group into No Man's Land with a fluttering newspaper tied to the top of his rifle as a flag of truce, and sent a letter about his experience to the *South Wales Weekly Argus*. 'I took some tobacco and jam to the Germans,' he began. 'But never no more. Another sergeant, a pal of mine from Monmouth, did the same, but when he was coming back to the trench they shot him through the back and killed him. He fell down and said, "My God, I'm done". They are dirty cowards, after [our] giving them tobacco.' Frank Collins had ventured, unarmed, to take packets of Woodbines to the Bavarians. The official notification was 'killed in action'. The Germans sent an apology across the line, but it could not have meant much to the 39-year-old postman's wife and three children.

Some Christmas casualties were the result of British provocations—accidental fire returned, a suspicious act responded to. Lieutenant Alfred Dougan Chater of the 2nd Gordons predicted in a letter home that 'the truce will probably go on until someone is foolish . . . We nearly messed it up this afternoon, by one of our fellows letting off his rifle skywards by mistake, but they did not seem to notice it so it did not matter.' Rifleman John Erskine of the 5th Cameronians wrote of a Regular in his regiment near Houplines who disobeyed an order to withhold fire while troops were meeting in the open. A German officer was hit. 'The Germans immediately replied and instead of firing on where the shot came from they evidently fired at the first person they saw. Unfortunately this happened to be one of our corporals who was shot through the head.' In territorial units, family groups often served together. 'A most regrettable fact connected with the affair,' Erskine understated, 'was that he has three brothers in this battalion, and it must have had a disheartening effect on them.' Walter Sinclair Smith died without regaining consciousness. An officer in the Westminsters, which relieved the Scots the next day, wrote, 'One of the German officers came over and apologized. It was a rotten mistake as the rifleman died.'

In other places, there was no need to worry about making such mistakes: the truce had never happened. Captain J. L. Jack of the 1st

Cameronians recalled with surprise in his diary on 13 January the 'extraordinary stories of unofficial Christmas truces with the enemy', as 'there was no truce on the front of my battalion'. On each flank of his kilted troops, the Welch Fusiliers and the Scottish Rifles enjoyed a holiday, but the belligerent Jack guessed that his unit faced die-hard Prussians—a convenient explanation for a career officer but for the reality that the troops opposite him were Saxons.

One *Landwehr* officer—serving in an equivalent to the Territorials—answered a British overture with an acid response that would have made the Kaiser proud

Gentlemen—You asked us yesterday temporarily to suspend hostilities and to become friends during Christmas . . . At the present time, when we have clearly recognized England's real character, we refuse to make any such agreement. Although we do not doubt that you are men of honour, every feeling of ours revolts against any friendly intercourse towards the subjects of a nation which for years has, in underhanded ways, sought the friendship of all other nations [but our own], so that with their help they might annihilate us; a nation . . . professing Christianity . . . whose greatest pleasure would be to see the political

166

disappearance and social eclipse of Germany.

Gentlemen, you are not, it is true, the responsible leaders of English politics, and so you are not directly responsible for their baseness; but all the same you are Englishmen, whose annihilation we consider to be our duty. We therefore request that you take such action as will prevent your mercenaries, whom you call 'soldiers', from approaching our trenches in the future.

At higher levels, both commands ordered the disruption of Christmas wherever their writ was effective. Obediently, artillerymen sometimes fired from unseen distances while weapons of lower calibre closer to the line remained largely quiet. A German biplane flew over the Channel toward Sheerness hoping to spoil Christmas in London but turned back in the fog after crossing the Essex coast. To no effect the British sent seven seaplanes over the North Sea to Cuxhaven, also fogbound. The French command tried to impair Christmas from the air by releasing two thousand *fléchettes*—five-inch steel darts—from their planes onto German troops near Nampoel, intending to create panic. The holiday flight was a failure, good only for a morale-boosting diagram of the inaccurate devices in newspapers. Quietly, their manufacture was abandoned.

Front-line officers of the 139th (Royal Saxon) Infantry Regiment knew the rules when they deliberately did not—'for the sake of caution', their history concedes—report the cease-fire to higher authority. Fraternization would cause few difficulties for most company-level officers on both sides, but one for whom it became awkward was Major Archibald Buchanan-Dunlop of the 1st Leicesters, who faced opposite their centre and right 'very vicious' troops they took to be Prussians. On their left, however, appeared to be Saxons—'jolly cheering fellows for the most part, and so it seems silly in the circumstances to be fighting them'. Since a battalion on his left was already out in the open with the Saxons, Buchanan-Dunlop permitted his men to follow. Late on Christmas Day he wrote to his wife that the Germans on his flank had 'drawn a line halfway between our left trenches and theirs', and exchanges of tobacco and newspapers were going on. 'Firing has practically stopped, and it's only when our men start repairing wire entanglements that they send along some warning shots.' Less than covertly, both sides were securing areas that were too hazardous to work on under fire, and each activity viewed with suspicion by one side or the other underlined the transience of the truce.

There were some, usually with careers in

mind, who stubbornly kept military priorities in focus. Late on Christmas afternoon one of the most senior British officers to experience the cease-fire at first hand got a good look at what he called 'an extraordinary state of affairs'—Brigadier Walter Congreve, VC, commander of the 18th Brigade (Captain Billy Congreve's father). It was 'the men' who had 'arranged a truce between themselves', he charged, absolving his own staff of blame, 'and all day long they have been walking about together singing and smoking. The officers also walked and smoked, even to a colonel.' The disappointed general hoped that 'at midnight, firing would [re-]commence'. A friend of Congreve's boasted that he had shared cigars 'with the best shot in the German Army, who . . . had killed more of us than any dozen others, but I know where his loophole is now and mean to down him tomorrow'.

That the unsanctioned *Brüderschaft* would break down was inescapable. The only question was whether the end would come with darkness and be determined by plan, or whether it would happen in unanticipated ways—stray shots, drunken altercations and general misunderstandings. The daily report of the 13th Westphalians, opposite the Garhwal Rifles, defended the continuing truce on grounds of advantage. Since it was also prudent to claim that the initiatives came from the other side, the opposite of the reality, the officers preparing the Westphalians' daily war-diary, C. Groos and W. von Rudloff, alleged, rather, as they prepared their report on Christmas night, that earlier in the day 'the English made attempts at fraternizing', and that the Germans, in proper Christmas spirit, responded amicably.

As troops drifted peaceably back to their lines in the early twilight, confessions of regret were audible. At Neuve-Chapelle, where many thousands on both sides would die in March, a German captain using more French than English remarked to Edward Hulse as soil was spaded over the last dead that it was a pity that such brave men should have fallen—'Les Braves, c'est bien dommage.' Hulse reported the elegy to his captain, George Paynter, who then crossed the line to talk to the Saxon Oberleutnant and to offer him a Scottish scarf. When the Saxon returned to the 15th Westphalians' trenches he felt awkward that he had not offered a quid pro quo, and dug into his own Christmas boxes. As darkness fell a German orderly arrived at the halfway mark and left a pair of fur-lined gloves for Paynter. He would have little chance to use them, taking a Blighty in March. Going to his aid, Hulse, then a captain, was shot and killed. He was twenty-five.

In other sectors, prearranged signals either warned men back or confirmed the close of the truce. The Queen's Westminsters fired high a Very flare—in most areas the only kind of firing reported. 'Altogether,' Percy Jones of the Westminsters summed up in his diary, 'we had a great day with our enemies, and [we] parted with much handshaking and mutual goodwill.' Rifleman George Eade of the 3rd London Rifles reported a German who had lived in London parting from him with, 'Today we have peace. Tomorrow you fight for your country; I fight for mine. Good luck.' Opposite the 2nd Borderers the Germans sang 'God Save the King' and from their trenches the Tommies offered three cheers.

In most cases the adversaries parted as friends in the manner of pugilists shaking hands before the opening bell, but there was always an undercurrent of wariness. West of St Yves, Private William Tapp of the 1st Warwicks observed pragmatically in his diary that the Saxons opposite 'say they are not going to fire again if we don't, but of course we must and shall do'. Yet he conceded that 'it doesn't seem right to be killing each other at Xmas time'. It was an attitude that would be parodied by a wit in the 63rd Division, who wrote,

> I do not wish to hurt you
> But (Bang!) I feel I must.
> It is a Christian virtue
> To lay you in the dust.
> You—(Zip! That bullet got you)

You're really better dead.
I'm sorry that I shot you—
Pray, let me hold your head.

Captain Armes of the 1st North Staffs arranged to have his men continue contacts with the enemy 'until dusk, when we go in[to our lines] again and have songs until 9 P.M., when "war" begins again. I wonder who will start the shooting? They say "fire in the air and we will", and such things, but of course it will start, and tomorrow we shall be at it hard, killing one another.'

Some units had negotiated unwritten truces into the next day. Since others were under orders to move into reserve Christmas night or the next morning, their replacements, with no emotional commitment to the stand-down, could not be guaranteed to hold their fire, nor could the enemy be made aware of troop dispositions—although Tommies reported many Saxons warning that the Prussians were coming. In gunner Herbert Sulzbach's 63rd (Frankfurt) Field Artillery, the concluding hour was set for ten o'clock—nine on the other side—when they were to relocate to the south. They moved off 'under a bright moonlit night, icy cold and sparkling with stars'. Few units wanted to restart the war. In Sergeant William Williamson's 2nd Devons, each side had 'played the game' and when darkness came 'each man stood at his post in dead

172

silence. We only fired 24 rounds during the night.' Even that was to ward off a German drunk at their wire.

On the Allied side, the revengeful French, at the command level, did their best to undo the German Christmas. On the Alsace front, General joffre chose noon on Christmas Day (1:00 P.M. for the Germans) as a suitable moment to interrupt Christmas dinners on the other side of what would prove to be intractable networks of barbed wire. The 57th and 66th Divisions were to attack heights in the Vosges from which enemy rail transport between Colmar and Mulhouse could be disrupted by artillery fire. Most of the 152nd Regiment of the 66th were killed or taken prisoner when the German 29th Brigade surrounded the village of Steinbach. A week later, after heavy losses on both sides—one French regiment lost 700 men—the *poilu* had retaken only a remnant of Steinbach in house-to-house fighting. The German trains kept running.

The French 56th Brigade in Picardy had prepared, under cover of the truce, an even more nasty surprise for the Germans. Sappers were set at eleven on Christmas night to ignite a fuse under the 800 kilos of explosives tunnelled below the advanced German trenches. It had been dark for hours and an informal cease-fire in the sector, although still holding, had expired with sunset. 'But, there

173

being a misfire,' the Brigade's account reported, 'the operation is recommenced and the explosion takes place at 23:45.' Although Christmas still had a quarter-hour to run on the French side, Berlin clocks ticked at forty-five minutes after midnight. Nevertheless, the Germans were not asleep. 'Immediately,' the 56th's diary confessed, 'a [French] detachment rushes forward to take possession of the crater and exploit the incident, but the enemy, being on the alert, greets them with rocket flares, hand grenades and above all rifle fire. Finally they execute a counter-attack and our detachment withdraws with some difficulty, using the bayonet.' No more literal case of being hoist with one's own petard occurred on the Western Front as Christmas Night ended.

In this unsystematic fashion, the truce was winding down. Yet it had not quite ended. The day after Christmas, Boxing Day, was a much-loved product of the English class system and the Victorian Christmas—a good excuse to extend the truce. In the 1840s, the family Christmas had become so crowded with churchgoing, festive feasting, visits to relatives and gift-giving among friends and loved ones that there was no holiday to be spared for the servants, for whom it was the most difficult day in the calendar. In the spirit of Victorian trickle-down magnanimity, a second and lesser Christmas was devised for St Stephen's Day, the day after. (The Germans also celebrated

174

St Stephen's Day as a *Zweiten Weihnachtsfeiertag*—a second and more ceremonial Christmas.) Household help and other service workers would each receive a 'Christmas Box'. Household staff often received, also, a half-holiday. Sometimes the 'box' was a gold sovereign, or a banknote in an envelope, but a 'Christmas Box' nevertheless. Thus Boxing Day. In the class-ridden British army it was almost as important an event as Christmas itself. The Germans were no less attached to their second Christmas.

Few units involved in the impromptu truce were eager to return to the war of attrition that seemed endless. Some had agreed to extend the cease-fire into a further day; a few held out for a New Year's conclusion to the truce. Headquarters on both sides responded with threats of punitive action. Local commanders, whipsawed between higher brass and men whose lives were literally on the line, argued that the continued lull furnished valuable time to drain flooded trenches, repair wire entanglements, and bring up ammunition and supplies. Reluctantly, many battalions on the line recommenced hostilities, if only perfunctorily. In the 1st Warwickshires, Private William Tapp noted, an officer cautioned the Germans opposite at 8:40 A.M. to return to their trenches, as British artillery had been ordered to begin shelling at nine. A German joked in return, 'We will get into your trenches as we shall be safer.'

'If you had only seen this mob [between the lines],' Captain F. D. Harris wrote to his family about Boxing Day, 'you would have thought you were dreaming.' But the truce had already become precarious. Shots were fired from somewhere on the Saxon side, and everyone scurried for cover. Soon a message was thrown over, on a piece of dirty cardboard attached to a stone: 'We shot in the air.' They had been ordered to fire. The happy milling about resumed, but Harris added in his letter, which his wife would send to a Liverpool paper, 'Of course, war is war, and I expect we shall be at it properly again in a short time.'

Even a token return to hostilities was usually preceded by a courteous signal to the other side. On the banks of the Lys, Captain Stockwell of the 2nd Welch Fusiliers had three shots fired high and harmlessly at 8:30 A.M., posted a sign reading 'MERRY CHRISTMAS' above a forward trench, and climbed atop his parapet. The Germans opposite quickly displayed a 'THANK YOU' sheet, and their company commander stood proudly on his own parapet. The two officers bowed, saluted, then descended into their trenches, from which the German captain fired two shots into the air. The war recommenced.

In a few places on the line, as during the day before, the shooting restarted less formally. In Victor Chapman's Foreign Legion unit, he wrote to his Uncle Willy, the men had orders not to fire, but the Germans began 'send[ing] over about a dozen an hour to let us know their presence'. In the renewed rain, 'wetness combined with filth' made 'a hard combination to be cheerful'. His section had at last a sort of shelter, a shallow trench barely three feet deep, 'and just room enough for all the men to lie in, provided they begin at the corner and range along head to feet like sardines'. It was far from a comfortable situation in which to remain for very long, and 'Nedime, a picturesque, childish Turk, began . . . standing on the trenches and yelling at the opposite side. Vesconsoledose, a cautious Portuguese, warned him not to expose himself so, and since he spoke German, [Nedime] made a few remarks [while] showing his head. He turned to get down and—fell! a bullet having entered the back of his skull: groans, a puddle of blood.'

Where the French and Germans had left their parapets without fear and exchanged chocolates and tobacco, a few shots began to be heard, then a rolling fire. A young German infantryman got up to dash from his trench and his companion warned, 'Stay here: the French will shoot you to pieces.'

'I left a box of cigars up there,' explained Fritz, 'and must have it back.' Another soldier also warned him to wait—that things would quiet down again. 'They won't hit me,' said

Fritz, 'I've been here three months, and they haven't caught me yet.'

He arose and tumbled back. 'Part of his brains was sticking to my belt,' his companion recalled. 'His cap flew high up into the air . . . The cigars were later fetched by another man.'

The following day an order was read out to their unit. 'We were forbidden to wear or have in our possession things of French origin; for every soldier who was found in possession of such things would be put before a court-martial as a marauder by the French if they captured him.'

When the writer recalled the episode in 1917 it was from New York. He had deserted into Holland and stowed away on a ship to America.

Little enthusiasm for hostile action remained in sectors where the truce had held. 'During the whole of Boxing Day,' Frank Richards wrote, the 2nd Welchs 'never fired a shot, and they'—the enemy—'the same; each side seemed to be waiting for the other to set the ball a-rolling. One of their men shouted across in English and inquired how we had enjoyed the beer. We shouted back and told him it was very weak but that we were grateful for it. We were conversing on and off during the whole of the day.'

Although most units were informed when they would be replaced in the line, the Welchs were relieved without notice late in the afternoon of Boxing Day by a battalion innocent of the truce, very likely because the appetite of the Fusiliers for fighting the men opposite had diminished. 'We were mighty surprised,' Richards recalled, 'as we had heard no whisper of any relief during the day. The men who relieved us . . . told us that from what they had been told the whole of the British troops in the line, with one or two exceptions, had mucked in with the enemy . . . They also told us that the French people had heard how we had spent Christmas . . . and were saying all manner of nasty things about the British Army.'

By now, most units faced resuming hostilities, however unwillingly. When the 107th Saxons cautioned the 1st North Staffs that shooting had to recommence, both sides showed authentic unwillingness. According to the Staffordshires' official history, on the morning of Boxing Day the commander of C Company learned that a German officer was waiting in No Man's Land to speak to him. 'On going out he found a very polite and spotless individual awaiting him, who, after an exchange of compliments, informed him that his Colonel had given orders for a renewal of hostilities at mid-day and might the men be warned to keep down, please?' The British captain thanked the *Hauptmann* for his courtesy, 'whereupon, saluting and bowing from the waist, he replied, "We are Saxons;

you are Anglo-Saxons; [the] word of a gentleman is for us as for you".'

The Staffs were duly warned to keep down. Just before the shooting was to restart, 'a tin was thrown into A Company lines with a piece of paper in it informing them, "We shoot [in]to the air", and sure enough at the appointed hour a few vague shots were fired high over the trenches. Then all was quiet again and the unofficial truce continued.'

Opposite the 1st Hampshires, the Saxons sent a message much like the one the Staffs received: 'Gentlemen, our automatic fire has been ordered from the Colonel to begin again at midnight; we take honour to award you of this fact.' The warning was not couched in the best English, but the attitude of the battalion commander was unmistakable. In the XIX Saxon Corps, which included the 107th, there was almost a mutiny in one regiment when it received orders to begin shooting again. According to the woman to whom the German sergeant told his story,

The difficulty began on the 26th, when the order to fire was given, for the men *struck*. Herr Lange says that in the accumulated years [of his service] he had never heard such language as the officers indulged in, while they stormed up and down, and got, as the only result, the answer, 'We can't—they are good fellows, and we can't.' Finally, the officers turned on the men with, 'Fire, or we do—and not at the *enemy*!' Not a shot had come from the other side, but at last they fired, and an answering fire came back, but not a man fell. 'We spent that day and the next,' said Herr Lange, 'wasting ammunition in trying to shoot the stars down from the sky.'

Even some troops that had exchanged heavy fire on Christmas Day had a more relaxed interval on Boxing Day. The Irish Guards, near Le Touquet with the Hertfordshires, had endured occasional but heavy shelling while trying to dig in positions vacated by three Indian units, the 4th Dogras, 6th Jats and 9th Gurkhas. Since the Indians were much shorter, their replacements had to dig the trenches deeper—wet and dreary labour until the freeze set in. Two officers and six men were wounded during the work and distribution of Christmas cards from Earl Kitchener, their honorary colonel, was a less than exhilarating event. Boxing Day was quieter but costlier. Four men were wounded that morning as they hacked at the hard ground and it was no consolation that the frost gave way locally to rain. Clods of clay stuck to their spades, and the trenches again began to fill with water. Troops had to stand on planks which rested on logs, with straw filling the gaps. Only the pollarded willows on the banks of the ditches thrived. Their top branches lopped back to the trunks to stimulate new growth, they had in some cases been pruned anew by gunfire.

In a few sectors where peaceability came late, the truce only occurred on Boxing Day or even later. On the morning of the 26th, Lieutenant Cyril Drummond of the Royal Field Artillery returned from reserve the night before and without front-line news other than his orders, set out with a telephone technician to begin spotting duties in an observation post set up for cover in a wrecked house at St Yvon, atop a slope north of Ploegsteert Wood. No firing could be heard as they walked toward the front lines, but the pair had not been prepared for what they saw. 'Looking down toward the trenches it was just like [an] Earl's Court Exhibition. [The vast Olympia in west London sometimes staged realistic, populous extravaganzas. One attended by Queen Victoria had been a city of Venice complete to canals with gondolas. Another attended by the Queen late in the old century had been Buffalo Bill's Wild West Show, with stagecoaches and a mock Indian raid with real Indians.] There were the two sets of opposing trenches only a few yards apart, and yet there were soldiers, both British and German, standing on top of them, digging or repairing the trench in some way without ever shooting at one another. It was an extraordinary

182

situation. And so my telephonist and I walked down the sunken road in full view of everybody in Germany, with no one taking any notice of us.'

Instinct took over and Drummond was soon exchanging souvenirs. 'They were nice fellows to look at,' he wrote with surprise after his diet of alarmist propaganda. One German explained the situation to Drummond as 'We don't want to kill you and you don't want to kill us. So why shoot?' Drummond hauled out his camera and shot a photograph instead, lining up nine assorted soldiers in his lens, in an assortment of uniforms, hats, and scarves. There was no need for him yet at that broken window in St Yvon.

The 1st Battalion of the Bavarian 16th Regiment, opposite the Manchesters and Devonshires, had spent Christmas night digging connective trenches between Messines and battalion headquarters. As they worked they could hear 'the whistling and stomping' of a small locomotive that was shuttling cars of British reinforcements to and from the line. The Bavarians had already been out fraternizing 'face to face' with the English on Christmas Day. Normally, wrote Private Rupert Frey of the 7th Company, 'we only knew of their presence when they sent us their iron greetings.' Now, 'from all sides', they gathered 'as if we were friends, as if we were brothers. Well, were we not, after all!' But

183

Frey's captain had now disapproved of the 'chumminess'—although they were not to fire 'unnecessarily'.

Corporal Josef Wenzl's 4th Company, in reserve earlier, moved up to the line. At three in the morning on the 26th, he wrote to his family, 'a star-bright night',—everything in the trenches which they occupied was 'frozen solid'. He expected to be fired on in the brilliant predawn light: 'We simply had to be spotted.' His unit dug in for heavy shelling. When nothing happened, the men they were relieving explained the quiet. They had been out the day before 'exchanging things with the English'—which Wenzl took as 'sheer lunacy'. But in his dugout he found English cigarettes, 'which I enjoyed very much'.

At first light both English and Germans left their trenches freely. Several Bavarians placed a *Weihnachtsbaum* they had brought with them on a parapet, lit its candles, 'and rang some bells'. Between the lines they 'pressed hands' with the enemy. 'The only star in the sky at nine o'clock in the morning'—eight English time—'was directly above them, which the men considered to be a special sign from heaven.' An Englishman borrowed an enemy harmonica and played while 'others' danced, and some Englishmen 'were colossally proud to wear German helmets on their heads'. And they sang carols both *'Freund and Feind'* knew. 'For the rest of my life,' Wenzl prophesied, 'I shall never forget this scene. Which goes to show that human feelings continue to go on even if, in these times, men do not know anything but killing and murdering.' But having survived into November 1916, Acting Sergeant Wenzl volunteered to fly and was shot down on 6 May 1917.

The 3rd Battalion of the 143rd Alsatians also had a delayed Christmas with the enemy despite a visit of the regimental band to play holiday music. The British of the 3rd Division, at the northernmost end of their line, had listened, and withheld fire, but only on the 'Second Christmas' did a member of Lieutenant Hans Bossert's company hold up a sign at his parapet reading *'Fröhliche Weihnachten'*. They had been busy using the holiday pause to dry out. The 143rd had one of the soggiest trench systems on their side of the line, which Bossert deplored as 'viscous mush'. Footbridges were below hanging cots made of wire and padded with tobacco leaves; sand sacks kept food reasonably dry and away from wet, black rats. At Christmas, with the help of *Pioniere*—engineering units—Lieutenant Colonel Bode, the battalion commander, had a drainage ditch built that vented the water towards the lower-lying enemy. A 'magnificent sign' with the inscription 'Bode Valley' marked their success.

According to the official history of the 143rd written by a Lieutenant Meinecke, following

185

their belated recognition of Christmas, 'The English immediately responded in like manner. A . . . soldier shouted to us in perfect German, asking if we wanted to remove the dead between the lines . . . We came to an agreement and some of our men climbed over the parapet, as also did some of the English . . . The sight of opposing troops chatting to each other along a stretch of several hundred metres was a very strange one.' They exchanged cigarettes and chocolate, and arranged to bury '50 to 60' bodies lying between the lines. They even sang together. But the suspicious Bossert claimed that he kept his machine guns quietly at the ready despite the 'busy to-and-fro', and at dusk both sides prudently returned to their trenches, recognizing the fading of the second Christmas.

A British Field Artillery lieutenant also late to the cease-fire was John Wedderburn-Maxwell, who had arrived at a position near Fauquissart on Christmas night and discovered only then what had gone on in his absence. He was 'terribly jealous', he wrote to his father, 'of having missed such an experience'. The next morning, Boxing Day, it was still quiet, and he went out to see whether the stand-down was continuing. As he got beyond the British wire entanglements and saw Germans wandering about unarmed, his supporting artillery, spotting them, too, opened up. The shelling was obviously unsynchronized with the Royal Irish Rifles, whom the gunners were supposed to be supporting. Wedderburn-Maxwell 'made a dash for our trench and [retreated] into it like a rabbit, but the "Allemands" didn't seem to mind tho' they went to ground for a few minutes and popped up later'.

At midday he crossed back into his own lines and reported for lunch with the battalion commander of the Irish Rifles, receiving the impression that friendly relations with the enemy were still possible. Now he was determined 'to hold a conversation', and taking a supply of cigarettes for barter, he set off with a corporal from his battery to the halfway point between the lines. Slipping past the wire, he gestured to some Germans hovering about their forward trenches to come forward, and they did—first two, then four more. One identified himself as a German-American, becoming spokesman and interpreter as the ritual exchanges took place. Wedderburn-Maxwell thought as they chatted that he had become part of 'probably the most extraordinary event of the whole war—a soldier's truce without any higher sanction by officers and generals, with firing going on to the right and rather further to the left. We strolled up and down for about half an hour, shook hands, said goodbye, saluted and returned to our lines.'

At St Yves, Private William Tapp, an

orderly in the 1st Warwicks who had tried to arrange a football game with the enemy but was more adept at cooking, went out to scrounge coal from a shattered house between the trenches 'where neither side dare go at ordinary times. I . . . meet a few Germans on the way, they have come to buy one of our army knives. I don't want to sell mine so we exchange coins. I have got 3, also five rounds of [German] ammunition. I give one pkt of cigarettes get cigars in return, then I go for the coal, a German comes with a bag to get some too, he helps me fill my bag so it was only polite to help him fill his, it didn't take long to clear all the coal out of that cottage . . . We could not have done that last time we were here. One fire would have caused volleys to be sent over.'

It was very likely unfriendly fire that claimed Corporal Ferguson of the 2nd Seaforths, the only man in his battalion wounded on Boxing Day. On Christmas Eve he had been celebrating with the Bavarians, and could not believe that they were guilty of maiming him. He blamed Boche artillery, also operating independently of the ground troops. Later, from a hospital in Nottingham—he had got his Blighty wound—he prepared diary extracts for publication in the *Saturday Review* by dictating copy to a nurse. For Boxing Day he recorded what would be his last action as a fighting soldier:

They have not fired yet, but the artillery have been busy, and they have the range of our trenches; they have started shelling on the right; word is passed along for our section to retire to reserve trenches. I had just left my mud hut to carry out the order . . . and the next shell I didn't know was going to strike me—but it did!

Ferguson lost an 'arm amputated at [the] elbow' and 'had six pieces of shrapnel and two bullets removed . . . I know it was not our new-made friends the Bavarians who shot me, but the artillery of the Prussians—the dogs'.

When General Sir Horace Smith-Dorrien of II Corps left his cushy headquarters on the evening of Boxing Day to examine the situation for himself, it was to check whether the maintenance of the offensive spirit, called for in his orders of 5 December, was being carried out. As he expected from disconcerting reports from the field, 'sufficient attention' indeed was not being paid to fighting the Germans. Yet he had been shrewdly directed to two points in the line where no actual mingling of adversaries was taking place. Anger at that unseen but not unknown phenomenon appeared, nevertheless, in Smith-Dorrien's confidential memorandum to his commanders:

I would add that, on my return, I was shown a report from one section of how, on Christmas Day, a friendly gathering had taken place of Germans and British on the neutral ground between the two lines, recounting that many officers had taken part in it. This is not only illustrative of the apathetic state we are gradually sinking into, apart also from illustrating that any orders I issue on the subject are useless, for I have issued the strictest orders that on no account is intercourse to be allowed between the opposing troops. To finish this war quickly, we must keep up the fighting spirit and do all we can to discourage friendly intercourse.

I am calling for particulars as to names of officers and units who took part in this Christmas gathering, with a view to disciplinary action.

Battalions were now being pulled back and replaced on the line, the departing troops suspecting that they were now considered unreliable. (Most shifts of personnel, however coincidental, were actually part of the clockwork schedule of time on the line followed by relief in reserve.) Both sides recognized how insubstantial the rapprochement had been. A two days' wonder, it had been a promising if frail start, in need of further nurture. As fresh troops took up positions on the line, only a downturn in the weather kept a semblance of the cease-fire in place.

Snow gave way to rain, turning the fields of Flanders once more into mud and slime. On both sides of the line, troops became too preoccupied with the sheer physical problems of maintaining waterlogged life in trench conditions to be eager to restart the war. Major Buchanan-Dunlop wrote to his wife that 'knee-deep' was not merely a figure of speech in such conditions, as a six-foot subaltern 'stuck so fast that he had to be pulled out by his men'. General Smith-Dorrien reported that 'two unfortunate Cameron Highlanders disappeared in a morass; one was never found and the other died on being recovered'. A young Field Artillery officer, he added, 'has also been lost in the same way'.

While miserable weather prolonged the truce toward the new year, both High Commands wanted to get on with the war, but that was not a practical matter, whatever the moral dilemmas were on the line. The British and French were the more anxious, as the Germans, sitting on large areas of occupied territory, could wait for Allied peace initiatives and home front disillusion in the West. But perhaps more important, many troops had discovered through the truce that the enemy, despite the best efforts of propagandists, were not monsters. Each side had encountered men much like themselves, drawn from the same walks of life—and led, alas, by professionals who saw the world through different lenses.

Many British and German soldiers, and line officers, viewed each other as gentlemen and men of honour. Violating the rules of war was treachery. Vera Brittain, who had worked as a nurse in France, reported an incident told by 'a Buxton officer home on sick-leave'. While the truce was ongoing, and troops on both sides took turns working along the line unmolested, 'the British company commander went sick, and a fire-eating patriot took his place. On the first occasion after his arrival that a group of Saxons left their trenches and placidly began their wire-mending, the fire-eater ordered his company's guns to be turned on them. The men had no choice but to obey, and a large number of benevolent Saxons were ignominiously wiped out.' In that sector the truce was obviously over.

Four out of five men, said her informant, 'roared with laughter' on being told about the attack by the officer from Buxton, and called it 'a smart piece of work'. So much, Brittain thought, for 'Hun atrocities'.

One French warning to the Germans, scrupulously honest, read, 'Be on guard tomorrow. A general is coming to visit our position. For reasons of shame and honour, we shall have to fire.' But Lieutenant Bolz wasted no Christian charity on the French. 'Such chummy overtures had taken place elsewhere, too. The strictest command was in force to respond immediately with hand grenades and rifle fire.'

On the morning after Boxing Day, thanks mostly to the weather, the pattern on the front remained one of tacit cease-fire in many areas. What Lieutenant John Wedderburn-Maxwell, who came late to it, on Christmas night, called 'a soldier's truce without any higher sanction by [field] officers and generals', was the shared feeling that the war would be decided at another place and time, and in another way— by some massive assault or by negotiations after a wearing down of the desire of governments to continue a wasteful conflict. Since men in the trenches saw themselves from their *Froschperspektive*—their frog's view—as only a sideshow which put them at useless risk, they preferred to make life at least marginally bearable. Troops on both sides had not reached the level of disproportion of cost and gain at which obedience to authority becomes untenable. Concerned, however, that such a point was approaching, the First Lord of the Admiralty, Winston Churchill, wrote acerbically to the Prime Minister, H. H. Asquith, on the day following Boxing Day, 'Are there not other alternatives than sending our armies to chew barbed wire in Flanders?'

Armies operated by discipline, and because chewing barbed wire was what authority demanded, no alternative existed. What high-ranking brass demanded was done. *'Die Schützengrabenfreundschaft verboten* (friendship between the trenches forbidden)' was the much regretted post-Christmas order from Spa. *'Fraternisieren'* the German High Command declared with obvious exasperation, was *'kein Sport'.* Sudden visits by opposing generals requiring a show of firing inevitably eroded further what was left of the truce even when the other side was quietly forewarned. 'We will remain your camarades,' went one message to the 2nd Yorks. 'If we shall be forced to fire we will fire too high.'

Unpredictability increased as the war reheated. On the 31st—St. Sylvester's Day to the Germans—a few English deaths from sniper fire were recorded. The day before the New Year had no priority, saint's day or not, to a committed sniper. Still, in some sectors a semblance of peace lasted into the new year. For the Scots, who gave 'Auld Lang Syne' to New Year tradition, the day preceding was Cake-day, or Hogmanay, when children called at nearby houses to solicit oatcakes, shouting the obscure, possibly Norman, words 'Hogmanay Trololay'—the cry for a New Year's gift. Like the more English Boxing Day, it was also an occasion for giving. Yorkshiremen, geographically close to the Scots, had a similar custom.

Major V. F. W. Dickins and his adjutant

made the rounds of the Queen Victoria's Rifles beginning at 10:30 P.M. on New Year's Eve, making their way

> through mud in many places over our knees. The night was fine and still, and quiet reigned on both sides. On arrival in the front trench we found the men very cheery but of course in a dirty and muddy state. The Germans could be heard singing hymns or songs . . . and all seemed fairly peaceful. We passed along the whole of our line, wishing the men a Happy New Year.

New Year's Eve also came to the fictional Private Schlump in sleepy Loffrande. Since his next assignment was inevitably the trenches, he hurried for some last jollity to the lively canteen at Fourbevilles. The *Stube* was filled with cigar smoke and the fumes of beer, over which artillerymen were becoming loudly merry. When the barrels of brew gave out, they drank liberated cognac out of their *Biersteine.* 'Before long, chairs and tables had been thrown down, and the sergeant major lay on the floor, snoring . .. . About midnight, [as] the men stormed out of the place, a tremendous cannonade came rolling southward; the men stumbled over to their quarters, brought out their carbines, and shot into the air like lunatics.' Although the tumult

195

was to welcome the New Year, Schlump groggily had no idea what was going on. A light snow was falling—a thin sheet that lay on the fields.

Little of the holiday mood remained. New troops on the line had no sense of being survivors. They prepared for their coming trials with doses of patriotic calls to arms. 'I saw the New Year last night,' the battalion CO, Lieutenant Colonel Wilfrid Smith, wrote, 'in the most depressing way, wet, cold, slush and bullets and rockets. The Germans sang carols, so our men shot at them to keep them quiet.' It was the end, Lieutenant Thomas of the 15th Westphalians recalled in 1934, of 'Christmas Peace'.

The end came, according to a tale allegedly told to Alexander Woollcott, an American army journalist in France in 1918, in quite another and more melodramatic way— perhaps a variant of the Buxton lieutenant's story. A former officer in the Warwickshires near Messines at Christmas 1914 described to Woollcott the slimy trenches and turnip fields, and the 'murmurous, jostling crowd' of troops without weapons engaged in 'monstrous disobedience involving the colossal defiance of the high and mighty'. On one flank, however, the officer recalled, a regiment of Highlanders 'eyed the proceedings dourly'. Some Fritzies and Tommies masqueraded happily in 'loot from abandoned French villages'—frilly finery, colourful parasols, and 'mouldy old silk hats' of the sort worn by local mayors. (Such incidents did occur.) But a British brigadier was 'most annoyed' at the indiscipline and ordered his troops back into their trenches.

As dusk was settling, the 'new friends' began returning to their lines, but with vows to re-gather for football the next morning. At dawn the Warwickshires subaltern was out of his dugout as fast as he could scramble. 'For all he could tell, the Highlanders were not typical . . . Something like this outburst [of fraternity] was taking place all along the line . . . If so the war was over. There would be, he thought, no authority on earth powerful enough to set those men fighting again.'

In the brightening dawn he could see the eager Germans swarming out of their trenches, 'the same jolly, unarmed lot of the day before . . . As they advanced, the Highlanders on the left opened fire and mowed them down.'

The Christmas truce, however, did not end that way. Highlander regiments participated while it lasted, and the reminiscence embroidered 'across a lobster stew at Billy the Oysterman's' seems a perverse myth to set opposite the snow-booted Cossacks and the Angels of Mons. The reality was less dramatic and involved renewed fire that was more desultory than deliberate. A German complaint would appear, in verse, in the

Plauener Sonntägs-Anzieger.

> *Die Englander schiessen so ins Blaue*
> *hinein, sie denken gar nicht, das da*
> *Leute konnten sein.*

> *[The English are shooting randomly into*
> *the blue;*
> *they don't stop to think that people might*
> *be there.]*

As a play, *Tunnel Trench* by Hubert Griffith, suggested, once the shooting began again, the old animosities would revive. ' 'Ave we 'ated you?' a Tommy asks a captured German. 'Not when you palled up with us Christmas 1914.' But as bellicosity on both sides boiled over, it was 'Gawd's 'oly bible truth' that 'as I'm alive, we'll lose our 'eads . . . [and] chuck bombs down yer dugouts an' laugh . . . We'll bayonet yer wounded . . . [and] we'll get ter killin' yer fer the love of killin' . . . Gawd knows why it is, but so it will be. 'Taint, and won't be, our fault, but so it will be.'

In the rival countries, just as the war resumed, citizens began learning, from soldiers' uncensored letters from the front in their newspapers, about the spontaneous truce that was no more. While dozens of papers began printing letters posted home by soldiers amazed at their experience, the writers themselves—those not returned to reserve—

198

were again exchanging fire.

As Bruce Bairnsfather conceded, 'It was too much to expect that a table would be suddenly wheeled out into No Man's Land, accompanied by English and German Ministers with fountain pens and documents, ready to sign PEACE.' The higher the official echelon, he realized, the more indignant officialdom became about the peaceable interval that had interrupted the war, right up to the uppermost HQ. The holiday having passed, 'and the respective soldiers having been sorted out, and put back into their proper slots in the ground, the war went on again. Bullets whizzed around that one-time meeting-place [between the lines], and sundry participants in that social gathering were laid out stiff on parapets, awaiting burial.' Field Marshal Sir John French's headquarters issued a bland statement that 'After a comparative lull, on account of the stormy weather, the Allies and the Germans are again actively engaged in Northern France and Belgium.'

In the sector where the dusky Garhwals had greeted the Westphalians on Christmas Eve, the 2nd Worcesters were again on the line, firing in earnest. New in their arsenal was 'Archibald'—a trench mortar improvised from a large iron drainpipe. It looped into the German lines Tickler's jam tins once fraternally offered the enemy but now stuffed with explosives and nails. A mean device, it

199

symbolized the shift back to a mean war, which, depending upon which troops were in the trenches, rekindled irregularly as the poor fighting weather in early January improved, and friendly relations further deteriorated. Five months into the war, although a million were already dead, the trenches remained graves for the living. On both sides in 1915 there would be more dead on any single day than yards gained in the entire year. And there would be nearly four more years of attrition— not to determine who was right, but who was left.

CHAPTER SEVEN

WHAT IF—?

The official British history of the war twelve years after downplayed Christmas 1914 as a minor episode that bore little resemblance to what had actually happened:

> During Christmas Day there was an informal suspension of arms during daylight on a few parts of the front, and a certain amount of fraternization. Where there had been recent fighting both sides took the opportunity of burying their dead lying in No Man's Land, and in

some places there was an exchange of small gifts and a little talk, the Germans expressing themselves confident of early victory. Before returning to their trenches both parties sang Christmas carols and soldier songs, each in its own language . . . There was to be an attempt to repeat this custom of old time warfare at Christmas 1915, but it was a small and isolated one, and the fraternization of 1914 was never repeated.

During the truce, the wary English press published nothing about what soldiers were describing excitedly in letters home as 'the Wonderful Day'. When, overseas, the *New York Times* reported incorrectly on the last day of the year, 'FOES IN TRENCHES SWAP PIES FOR WINE', the unspoken embargo ended. Cable and telegraph spread the news quickly. The London *Daily News* would repeat the story. Letters from Tommies and Fritzes began appearing in uncensored home newspapers. On 8 January, 1915, the front page of the London *Daily Mirror,* and other newspapers, carried the first of the photographs with which servicemen accompanied their mail home, the *Mirror* displaying a happy mixed throng as AN HISTORIC GROUP'.

In the first week of the new year, dispatches, letters home, and press commentaries proliferated across Britain and even more cautious but curious Germany. (French censorship kept most stories from the papers.) The *South Wales Echo* on 1 January, 1915, predicted sweepingly, 'When the history of the war is written, one of the episodes which chroniclers will seize upon as one of its most surprising features will undoubtedly be the manner in which the foes celebrated Christmas. How they fraternized in each other's trenches, played football, rode races, held sing-songs, and scrupulously adhered to their unofficial truce will certainly go down as one of the greatest surprises of a surprising war.' The *Daily Mirror* on 2 January seemed almost treasonable in an editorial alleging that wartime hostility was to be found 'mainly at home', and that 'the gospel of hate' was difficult to embrace on the front lines 'when chance throws men into a companionship of toil and danger':

> The soldier's heart rarely has any hatred in it. He goes out to fight because that is his job. What came before—the causes of the war and the why and wherefore— bother him little. He fights for his country and against his country's enemies. Collectively, they are to be condemned and blown to pieces. Individually, he knows they're not bad sorts . . . The soldier has other things to think about.

He has to work and win. Consequently he has not time for rage, and blind furies only overwhelm him when the blood is up over fierce tussles in the heat of the thing. At other times the insane childishness is apparent to him . . . But now an end to the truce. The news, bad and good, begins again. 1915 darkens over. Again we who watch have to mourn many of our finest men. The lull is finished. The absurdity and the tragedy renew themselves.

The Times even published a letter from a German lieutenant—perhaps given to the other side to post—and editorialized on 4 January that, 'as the wonderful scenes in the trenches show, there is no malice on our side, and none in many of those who have been marshalled against us'. But cautiously limiting the significance of the cease-fire, the Edinburgh *Scotsman* the day before had seen it only as little more than a revival of the medieval 'truce of God'—a pause to observe religious rites.

German press coverage—even columns lifted from English papers—was more guarded. Despite dozens of firsthand reports in the press, a Leipzig magazine, *Reclams Universum*, downplayed the episode as of limited scope—'a great exaggeration' unrepresentative of the entire front, and empty of 'orgies of brotherly love'. Such expressions, soldier or civilian, it contended, could endanger the state. The magazine reprinted three pictures from London papers showing artists' depictions of warm fraternization and claimed that German accounts 'proved' that the enemy drawings were falsehoods. Both sides, however, had photographs of the real thing, these kept from illustrated weeklies in Germany.

Despite concessions that something did happen, in Berlin the *Tägliche Rundschau* was even more blunt. 'War is no sport,' it reminded Germans on New Year's Day, 'and we are sorry to say that those who made these overtures or took part in them did not clearly understand the gravity of the situation.' The military on 29 December had reaffirmed rules forbidding fraternization, tantamount to high treason. The war was not yet won.

Yet it might have already been lost. German strategy had been to outflank the French—and possibly the British as well—by sweeping through Flanders and enveloping Paris within forty-two days after mobilization. The plan for quick victory allowed for no untoward complications, and when the army had been halted at the Marne in September 1914 and turned back into Flanders, the feared long war of attrition would leave Germany and its unstable allies at disadvantages which could only worsen. But the spontaneous Christmas

Waffenstillstand had opened unanticipated options for both sides. Although the Germans could gain by a truce in place, no one chanced exploring the opportunity, even covertly. The culture of belligerence in Berlin made a cease-fire with unpredictable consequences *ausgeschlossen*—unthinkable.

The possibility was equally unthinkable on the other side. As controversial playwright George Bernard Shaw wrote (through neutral Switzerland) to his fire-eating German translator, Siegfried Trebitsch, on 19 January, 1915, 'It is all hallucination, this war spirit; we all talk nonsense. German papers, French papers, English papers write the same article word for word (except the names), tell the same lies, believe the same impossible stories.' Still, what had happened at Christmas had momentarily undermined flag-waving rhetoric. 'You said in your letter,' Shaw continued, 'that every German would hate England until she is destroyed. Yet, two days before you wrote these words German and English soldiers upset their officers by leaving their trenches to talk and smoke and play soccer ball with each other.' A future general, Captain Jack of the Cameronians, averse to the truce when on the line, had speculated in his diary a few days earlier, in almost Shavian fashion, about the larger implications of the cease-fire, which had extended farther than governments conceded, 'It is interesting to visualize the close of a campaign owing to the opposing armies—neither of them defeated—having become too friendly to continue the fight.'

The erosion of the 1914 truce as weather improved and unblooded units moved into the line had closed off the last practical opening for negotiating an abbreviated war. It was not that troops in the trenches, condemned to costly stalemate, wanted to fight on, but that their governments did. The Chinese writer Lu Xun once observed, wryly, 'Whoever *was* in power wishes for a restoration. Whoever is now in power is in favour of the status quo.' The Belgians, who had little left of their country, occupied seventeen miles of front. The British occupied little more than thirty miles, but they were the fulcrum of the active front. The French held the many southern miles of their line, to the Swiss border, but much of it, even opposite Alsace and Lorraine, lost in 1870, was—but for the barking of their symbolic 75s and a few misguided operations—as inactive in December as if it were peacetime. Despite official denials, and difficulties made by commanders, there had been considerable fraternization by the French in areas where real fighting had occurred, while in the south there wasn't much fight in the older reservists along the line.

A peace in place, nevertheless, seemed as impossible for the Western Allies as for the tottering Czarist regime in the east. The

Belgians and French could not concede the lost national territory, and the British had treaty obligations to its allies. The Germans could not give its seizures back without risking the collapse of their regime and its privileged Prussian ruling class. What the men doing the dying thought was irrelevant. They were under military discipline.

But what if—? Had the war ended abruptly with the Christmas truce [Before the truce, which surprised the Germans, a proposed *Kaiserliche* 'redistribution of Europe' had been leaked by Professor Ernest Haeckel of the University of Jena. The details, complete to a 'postwar' map, appeared as the lead article in the January 1915 issue of *Vanity Fair* in New York. Among other dispositions it involved 'the elimination of Belgium; the withdrawal from Russia of her Baltic provinces . . . the creation of a United Poland, under Austro-Hungary; the addition to Germany of Northeast France; the temporary occupation of London; the neutralization of the English Channel, and the annexation of [Russian] Finland to Sweden.' The article also speculated that with German hopes for a quick war dashed at the Marne, the Allies themselves might 'conquer' Germany 'some time in 1915' and reverse the settlement in the other direction.] one enters the fantasy world of alternative history. It is an intriguing and illuminating, yet dangerous place to visit.

Much evil would have been avoided by a world war ended early. Only the stalemate, and the certainty of a prolonged war, tempted the British into the catastrophic gamble at Gallipoli—proposed by the Committee of Imperial Defence's secretary, Colonel Maurice Hankey, as an alternative field of operations. The butchery in which hundreds of thousands of bodies were ground into the mud of the Western Front, leaving not an identifiable bone, would not have happened. The more than six thousand deaths every day over forty-six further months of war would not have occurred.

Bolshevism might have been a failed movement if led without Vladimir Lenin, an obscure, bookish radical in Zurich until slipped into Russia in 1917 by the Germans; and Russia, shorn of its western empire, independent nations now, from Finland to the Black Sea, might have regained the stability to evolve into a constitutional monarchy under a puppet Czar, or—following a weakened Czar's abdication—might have found its path to a moderate alternative to Sovietism. Fear of militant Bolshevism had much to do with the ruinous success of Rightist politics across Europe in 1918 and after. A post-Franz Joseph Austria-Hungary—the doddering old Emperor would die in 1916—might have separated more peaceably into a loose federation of nationalities, along, perhaps, with a reunified (possibly German-dominated) Poland; yet Slav states in the Balkans might still have suffered developmental disasters because of the militancy of restless populations.

There would have been no way the Germans could punish troops who would not take up arms again. There would have been too many of them—a potent political force. Instead, Germany might have become a prosperous, mildly socialist, constitutional Wilhelmine monarchy—in time, a republic— with Hitler an obscure demobilized corporal in a sea of discharged soldiers for whom the industrious nation would have found postwar work. The catastrophe of post-Versailles inflation need not have happened, nor its devastating economic political aftermath.

While rescuing its financial clout in Europe, Britain might have also rescued all or most of its colonies in Africa, where it was having some initial successes against the Germans. But burdened by its empire and by obsolescing infrastructure, Britain was on the edge of unrealized decline, exacerbated by the economic and manpower attrition of the long war. Ending the war sooner, even with some embarrassment, might have staved off temporarily the erosion of its position. Yet Germany had made it clear to Britain just as the war began, before the British intervened on behalf of Belgium and France, that it wanted 'a continuous Central African colonial empire'. Linking its eastern and western colonies with French cessions, if not British ones, across the equatorial waist of the continent, and—as the ultimate blackmail for evacuating Belgium [The German General Staff actually proposed offering France its invaded lands back if Belgium became a German protectorate.]—acquiring, as its centrepiece, the vast Congo, Germany (through negotiation) might have become the major power on the continent. South Africa, where the Boers had lost the war but not the peace, would become increasingly Afrikaner and anti-British, and inevitably ally with a Greater German Africa that would dominate the continent south of the Sahara. With the crucial veins of gold and pipes of diamonds beneath the Johannesberg Rand at indirect German disposal, a world on the gold standard with its luxury trade pivoted upon diamonds would fall under even greater Teutonic sway. (Yet that territorial aggrandizement might have appeared as a huge, unanticipated blunder a generation or two later, as Africa became more burden than bargain.)

While reoccupying its portion of Flanders, a wounded, festering France would not have regained Alsace and Lorraine, and might have turned—it nearly did anyway—into a Fascist, revanchist state nursing grievances for yet another war it could not win. Anti-semitism, in temporary retreat after the implosion of the

Dreyfus affair, would have revived as the French scrounged for scapegoats. And the ostrich-like Maginot Line mentality into which the French retreated in imagined triumph after 1918 might have been more extreme in 1915. France would have lost in victory or in defeat.

New Arab states might have split off more deliberately and less violently from an undefeated but decadent Turkey, inevitably to relinquish an empire the doomed sultanate could not control. A late product of the war, Kemal Ataturk would not have arisen to rejuvenate Turkey, the 'sick man of Europe'. While it could still do so, however, it might have entertained ideas (at its profit) from an increasingly affluent European Jewish population, spared a Holocaust, to settle (at the start) a modest number of Zionists to farm portions of Palestine, perhaps into vineyards and citrus groves. With no Balfour Declaration by Britain in 1917, a very different Israel might have had an earlier birth.

Japan would have lost the opportunity to seize German colonies in the Pacific, but would make up for that greedily by massive moves into China (as it did, anyway, later) and into Southeast Asia; and a war on the Pacific rim might have happened much as it did and when it did. Japan would have moved against Britain, France and the Netherlands in Southeast Asia much as in 1941, only sooner.

Perhaps the United States in the Philippines would have been spared for the moment and the Pearl Harbor sneak attack—mounted to restrain American intervention—rendered unnecessary, or postponed. A militarily weak United States, never to be drawn into the European war, might have sunk into deeper political isolation in its own hemisphere—even into technological isolation. And the idealistic Wilsonian political impracticalities for Europe might never have been incubated.

If the American postwar cycle of isolationism had then been succeeded by its opposite, a different historical momentum for the United States might have followed. Westward expansion into the Pacific, to link the Philippines with Hawaii, might have precipitated conflict with Japan. Rejecting Europe, Americans might have entertained long dormant designs about expanding into weakly populated and militarily insignificant western Canada, to link up with Alaska, and into the isolated appendage of the Maritime Provinces, to link up with New England, while France, seeking a source of pride unavailable in Europe, might have attempted to destabilize and detach Quebec, a dream not quite dead. The longer war helped solidify Canada into a nation it might not have been otherwise.

With the long war responsible for so many quantum jumps in engineering, the tank might have been slower to develop, and aircraft and rocket development would have been slowed, as Germany would not have pressed ahead with alternatives to aircraft denied them by Versailles in 1919. Germany's grand Zeppelin era, stimulated by the war but abruptly closed by the hydrogen explosion of the *Hindenburg*, might have lasted longer. (Because its success would have assisted the Nazi regime, the great cruise liners of the air had been denied safer helium by the United States in the 1930s.) Jet and rocket engines would have been developed anyway, but without economic or military incentives to accelerate the pace of their technology. Germany's primary naval weapon, the submarine, would have gained impetus from spectacular early wartime successes. Would there have been a pioneering German nuclear sub fleet later?

Nuclear fission would have been discovered more or less when it was, about 1938, but only military urgencies would have accelerated its use as a power source, and its strategic applications. The refugee scientists so much a part of the American breakthroughs in physics and chemistry might have remained productively at home in central Europe. With so many brilliant physicists in Germany, and even Japan (as we now know), atomic weapons theory and nuclear energy and propulsion devices would have matured in many places, especially in Germany, but only war necessities would have encouraged the financing needed for the hardware.

Yet America would not have slipped into scientific isolation. The United States was already the leading nation in engineering and in the applications of electricity. Although spurred by war, radio and television would have developed anyway, along with the vacuum tube, which expanded their possibilities. Peaceable pursuits like astronomy might have benefited, and biological research given stronger impetus. Medicine, especially surgery, often quickened by war, might have found different directions, and the applications of antibiotics delayed. Penicillin and the sulpha drugs were already being worked out in the laboratories, but only war promoted mass production.

Germany in peace rather than war would have become the dominant nation in Europe, possibly in the world, competitor to a more slowly awakening America, and to an increasingly ambitious and militant Japan. No Wilsonian League of Nations would have emerged to provide bitter lessons, some unlearned, for a future, different, and more belated United Nations. Yet a relatively benign, German-led, commonwealth of Europe might have developed decades earlier than the European Community under leaders not destroyed in the war or its aftermath. Among Germany's secret proposals to Britain had been a 'central European economic association' with common customs treaties to 'stabilise Germany's economic dominance over *Mitteleuropa.*' That would have been much easier before four draining years of war made both victors and vanquished embittered debtors to the sole creditor nation, the United States.

With, very likely, no Lenin or Stalin or Trotsky, and no Hitler or Mussolini (another upstart product of the war), the faces of politics would be very different: but for one. Churchill, already on the rise and—thanks to the Christmas Truce, if it succeeded— unembarrassed by Gallipoli, might have achieved his ambitions sooner, while Franklin D. Roosevelt, only an obscure assistant secretary of the navy—of a fleet going nowhere militarily—would have returned to a boring law practice, and never have been the losing but attractive vice presidential candidate in 1920, a role earned by his war visibility. Wilson, who would not be campaigning for re-election in 1916 on a platform that he kept America out of war, would have lost (he only won narrowly) to a powerful new Republican president, Charles Evans Hughes, sparing the US electorate Harding and Coolidge and Hoover. A 'business' president after Hughes, however, might have been Henry Ford or Harvey Firestone. Douglas MacArthur, despite his ambitious mother's lobbying of the military bureaucracy in Washington, would have had far less opportunity to become the youngest general in the American army; Dwight Eisenhower, only a captain in a service reduced further by budget cuts, might have had to retire into civilian insignificance; a weekend Missouri National Guard artilleryman, Harry Truman, would have had only an unprosperous shop in a small town, and without a war record, perhaps no leverage into local politics.

Worldwide, one of the big losers in an abbreviated war would have been women. Deprived of the opportunity to replace men in the workforce on a large scale, they would not have had suffrage-focused promissory notes about equal social and legal rights, including the vote, to cash in. Such unfulfilled aspirations, if further delayed, inevitably would have led to more social tension and more violence, especially in Britain and probably elsewhere as well, including the United States.

In the arts, the American postwar expatriate community populated so vitally by war veterans who had experienced something of France, and returned, would not have existed, keeping culture at home more inward. In Europe itself, Cubism, forced into the shadows by war, would have re-emerged strongly, as would Bauhaus architecture and design, and Germany would have become the centre of culture (as well as science) rather than a weak and listless France. The war had interrupted and irreparably altered one of the most explosively creative periods in European life.

Much of this speculation may be frivolous, yet there can be no doubt that this 'what if' exercise hinges upon one of the twentieth century's most potentially significant events. The Christmas Truce reverberates with an incalculable sense of loss. The waste of the best talents in all warring nations was especially grievous, dramatically shown by the delayed appearance in England in 1915 of the annual edition of *Debrett's Peerage*. So many sons of the most energetic of the aristocracy were dead, Lyn Macdonald has written, 'so many baronets, and lords, and knights, so many heirs to great lands and titles had [already] been killed, that it took the editors many months to revise the entries of almost every blue-blooded family in the United Kingdom'. What would the most creative and productive lives spared everywhere have accomplished? What would their unborn children [Recall Walter Flex's mystical *Weihnachtsmärchen* with its otherworldly land of the unborn war-dead.] whose opportunities would have been enormous, have meant to the future? Would it have been a world worth the very different peace?

During a House of Commons debate on 31 March, 1930, Sir H. Kingsley Wood, a Cabinet Minister during the next war, and a major 'in the front trenches' at Christmas 1914, recalled that he 'took part in what was well known at the time as a truce. We went over in front of the trenches, and shook hands with many of our German enemies. A great number of people [now] think we did something that was degrading.' Refusing to presume that, he went on, 'The fact is that we did it, and I then came to the conclusion that I have held very firmly ever since, that if we had been left to ourselves there would never have been another shot fired. For a fortnight the truce went on. We were on the most friendly terms, and it was only the fact that we were being controlled by others that made it necessary for us to start trying to shoot one another again.' He blamed the resumption of the war on 'the grip of a political system which was bad, and I and others who were there at the time determined there and then never to rest . . . until we had seen whether we could change it.' But they could not.

A year after the thwarted truce, following much bloodshed and the loss of many of the soldiers on both sides who had shaken hands at Christmas 1914, the front in Flanders had shifted, soldier-novelist Wilfrid Ewart of the Scots Guards wrote, 'only a few hundred yards'. The field of battle had become 'only a little grimmer, a little more gashed with shell-holes, a little more torn and rent with trenches dug and trenches blown outward . . . a little

218

more haunted and possessed by the ghosts of the slain'. In the months between, further efforts to stop the shooting had failed. The day before Good Friday had been relatively quiet, and on Easter Sunday, 4 April, 1915, the Germans opposite the Sherwood Foresters raised a white flag and began leaving their trenches, but the British warned they would fire. In November a small fraternization occurred near St Éloi, south of Ypres, again initiated by the Saxons and responded to by the Liverpools. It quickly flickered out.

That December, to inhibit any pre-Christmas 'slackness' in discipline, the British command ordered a slow, continuing artillery barrage through every daylight hour. Despite the waste of lives on both sides, it also ordered trench raids by night and unsettling mortar bombardments by day. Yet there were some lapses, again with the 1st Scots Guards, the now-dead Hulse's unit, participating in singing and bantering across the trenches. But commanders were less forgiving, and there was at least one truce-related British court-martial proceeding in 1915.

From the command standpoint, conspicuous examples had to be made, and targeted for trial were the acting commander of the 1st Scots Guards, Captain Miles Barnes, and one of his company officers, Captain Sir Iain Colquhoun. On Christmas Day, Colquhoun had acquiesced in a cease-fire to bury the

219

dead. For a half-hour afterwards, the troops mingled. Then Colquhoun 'blew a whistle and both sides returned to their trenches. For the rest of the day the Germans walked about and sat on their parapets. Our men did much the same, but remained in their trenches. Not a shot was fired.'

Learning of the incident, Major General Lord Cavan, who did not know the difference between *explicit* and *implicit*, ordered an inquiry as to how 'my implicit orders came to be disobeyed'. The court-martial convened on 18 January, 1916, and Barnes, who was not directly involved, was cleared. Colquhoun was not. Seven decades later, the folksinger-composer John McCutcheon wrote and performed a ballad, 'Christmas in the Trenches', which he claimed was 'based on a true story from the lines of World War I'. He associated it with the 1914 truce and added, 'Ian Calhoun, a Scot, was the commanding officer of the British forces involved in this story.' He was charged with 'consorting with the enemy' and sentenced to death. 'Only George V spared him from that fate.'

McCutcheon's background history was melodramatically inaccurate on almost every count. The court-martial of Sir Iain Colquhoun had ended in a 'reprimand'—the mildest punishment possible. It was promptly remitted by General Haig. Captain Colquhoun returned to duty and rose through the war to brigadier general. Yet the ballad about his unit, ostensibly sung by a Private Francis Tolliver of Liverpool, described movingly and realistically the brief 'respite from the war' in the familiar images of silent guns and 'Silent Night', soccer-playing and exchanges of souvenirs.

As daylight again comes, and troops in the ballad reluctantly say their farewells to the enemy and 'settle back' to kill each other—in the ballad's 'what-if' idealism

> . . . the walls they kept between us to exact the work of war
> Had been crumbled and were gone forevermore.

At the least, Tolliver has learned, as he wonders 'whose family' he would be fixing in the sights of his gun, that

> The ones who call the shots won't be among the dead and lame,
> And on each end of the rifle we're the same.

However erroneous the song's specifics were, the conclusions were not. That recognition occurs at some moment in every war, as an Australian trooper remembered in North Africa late in 1941. At Tobruk, on the edge of the Libyan desert, rain fell for the first time since the siege of the wreck-strewn port began, and '[every] weapon-pit and latrine filled up with water like a huge drain'. Around the perimeter came a flood of debris (and remains of the dead) that had been collecting for half a year, and soldiers on both sides became too sodden and preoccupied to fight. The next morning, for a few hours, men on both sides openly stood up, in the past an invitation to be shot. They dried their clothes, made tea, and did not return desultory fire. An infantryman looking unnaturally old after months of exposure to the cruel sun, the dust and the strain, looked across at the enemy, who were suffering in the same way, and said to no one in particular, 'Nobody said we couldn't like them, they just said we had to kill them. All a bit stupid, isn't it?' Graham Greene explained it in writing about a very different kind of conflict in a different place and time. An enemy,' he wrote in his novel *The Human Factor* (1978), 'had to remain a caricature if he was to be kept at a safe distance: an enemy should never come alive. The generals were right—no Christmas cheer ought to be exchanged between the trenches.'

The Christmas Truce has lingered strikingly in the memory even when its details have disappeared into myth. What began as 'the Wonderful Day' to its participants remains a potent stimulus to the creative memory. Christmas 1914 evokes the stubborn humanity within us, and suggests an unrealized potential to burst its seams and rewrite a century. It lives also in the sardonic soldier exchanges in *Oh What a Lovely War!* and even in the fantasy encounters of the intrepid Snoopy with the Red Baron, in which chivalry wins out for a brief moment over rivalry. Its mood is recaptured in Great-Grandfather's saga of the innocent idealism of the heroic marzipan confectioner, Alfred Kornitzke, and in the warm, intense camaraderie of improvised between-the-trenches kickabouts. Although the unchanged reality of war is that the shots ordered by increasingly remote presences are absorbed by ordinary humans, Christmas 1914 reopened imaginations to the unsettling truth that at each end of the rifle, men were indeed the same.

Only a few failed attempts at a truce occurred in 1916 and 1917. But as New Year's Day came in 1918 the commanding officer of the 1st Hampshires noted in his diary, 'Enemy attempted to fraternize on our left, but were shot at by us, otherwise a quiet day.' Casualties had become so vast by mid-April in 1917 that mutinous *poilu*, in division strength, refused to return to the trenches on one French front at Aisne. What officialdom later downplayed as 'collective indiscipline' would be suppressed, and lead to 3,427 court martials and 554 death sentences unreported in censored French newspapers. (Only forty-nine soldiers—fifty-three by other accounts—were actually shot.) Germans, too, in regimental numbers, refused to return to the front. In *A Fable* (1954), William Faulkner would invent cryptically, perhaps with the actual events in mind, a surrealistic vision of a spontaneous armistice in the field at Easter 1918—'that curious week's holiday which the war had taken which had been so false that they remembered it only as a phenomenon'. In the novel a French regiment refuses to carry out a suicidal attack and a day later its disobedience has spread across the front—an impromptu recess in the war. But as had happened at Aisne (rather than, as popular memory has it, at Verdun), Faulkner's Passion Week fable ends with savage punishment of the peacemakers, after which the carnage continues.

The following November, forty-six months after the abortive truce, the war ground to an end. Still on occupied soil, to their perverse pride, everywhere along the Western Front, the exhausted Germans capitulated. Following the final Armistice came an imposed peace in 1919 that created new instabilities ensuring another war.

However much the momentary peace of 1914 evidenced the desire of the combatants to live in amity with one another, it was doomed from the start by the realities beyond the trenches. As the English rock band The Farm, decades later, summed up the results after the enemies 'joined together and decided not to fight', but failed, there was 'nothing learned and nothing gained'.

A celebration of the human spirit, the Christmas Truce remains a moving manifestation of the absurdities of war. A very minor Scottish poet of Great War vintage, Frederick Niven, may have got it right in his 'A Carol from Flanders', which closed,

> O ye who read this truthful rime
> From Flanders, kneel and say:
> *God speed the time when every day*
> *Shall be as Christmas Day.*

SOURCES

The sources indicated below chapter by chapter do not include documentation clearly identified in the text. Nor are general histories of the war cited except where something is quoted from a document possibly unavailable elsewhere. Most newspaper accounts in English may be found in the files of the British Newspaper Library, Colindale (London). Accounts in other languages are from scattered locations in Germany, Belgium and France. Some unique material is derived from the remarkable In Flanders Fields Museum, Lakenhallen, Grote Markt 34, Ieper, Belgium, which only opened its doors in April 1998. It holds promise to be a major location for the documentation of the war in Flanders, 1914–1918. As a source it is abbreviated below as IFF. The Imperial War Museum (London) is IWM. Many but not all of its Christmas Truce manuscript sources are indexed as such, and these furnish the core of the seminal *Christmas Truce,* by Malcolm Brown and Shirley Seaton (1984; revised edition London, 1994), here CT.

One valuable source of data has been the war diary—not the individual journals kept, often scrappily, given trench conditions, but the official war diaries of individual units, akin to the logs of ships. Another has been the personal letter from the front. Many quickly turned up in print because of the astonishing events recounted, and the astonishingly rapid postal service. Dozens of letters-to-the-editor in British newspapers from serving soldiers, almost always submitted by their families, can be located by diligent searching in the Newspaper Library at Colindale, London. (Many letters quoted here are from the Colindale archives, but some newspapers not on microfilm are rapidly deteriorating.) Equivalent German letters, surprising in their abundance, and which found their way into the press despite official displeasure, are scattered among the newspaper collections of many city and university libraries. World War II bombings have caused irrecoverable losses in this area of documentation, even more so in Germany than in England. The most fertile source for other German wartime data is the *Militärarchiv* of the Bundesarchiv, 79024 Freiburg, Germany.

Place name spellings will differ in quotations from English, Belgian, French and German sources (Dixmude, Dixmuide; Mesen, Messines, Iepar, Ypres etc).

INTRODUCTION

A much-publicized photograph, 'Regiments of Russians Welcomed in France', showing infantrymen debarking in Marseilles early in the war, appears in *Collier's Photographic History of the European War* (New York, 1916). The editorial paragraph on a possible Christmas truce in *The New Republic,* 26 December, 1914, is untitled on the first page of text. The 'Khaki Chums' re-enactment in 1999 is described by Taff Gillingham, one of the participants, on an illustrated Internet Web site, 15 June, 2000, which can be accessed as 'www.hellfirecorner.demon.co.uk/chums.htm.'

1. AN OUTBREAK OF PEACE

The officer in the 143rd is Hans Bossert, editor of *We, the 143rd: The 4th Lower-Alsatian Infantry Regiment No. 143 during Peacetime and during the World War, I* (Berlin, 1935). Ludwig Renn is quoted from his *Krieg* (Berlin, 1928). Charles Sorley is quoted from his *Letters* (London, 1919). Leslie Walkinton wrote to his parents on 26 December, 1914 (IWM). (Remarkably, he survived into the final armistice in November 1918: see S. Weintraub, *A Stillness Heard Round the World. The End of the Great War* [New York and London, 1985]) Geoffrey Heinekey is quoted from his diary entry of 27 December, 1914 (IWM). Rudolf Binding's letter to his father is in his *A Fatalist at War*, originally *Aus dem Krieg* (Berlin, 1925), trans. (Boston, 1929)

Ian F. D. Morrow. Valentine Williams described Flanders in 'Greatest of All Tributes to Christmas', *New York Times Magazine*, 23 December, 1934. Lyrics of 'The Old Barbed Wire' are from John Brophy and Eric Partridge, *The Long Trail: What the British Soldier Sang and Said in 1914–1918* (New York, 1965). Henry Williamson wrote of his emotional postwar visit to the Flanders graves in *The Wet Flanders Plain* (New York, 1929).

Data from the Imperial War Museum on the Princess Mary's Soldiers' and Sailors' Fund gift distributions is from Bette Dickinson via Lucy Addington. A brass Princess Mary Christmas Box itself came from Michel Pharand. Percy H. Jones is quoted from letters to his family typed sequentially as a diary (CT). Major G. D. Jeffreys is quoted from his diary in *Fifteen Rounds a Minute* (London, 1974). The mock-injuries suffered from the excess of gifts of food are described in *'Kleines Feuilleton', Frankfurter Zeitung,* 31 December, 1914. *'Notschrei . . .'* appeared in both English and in the original German verse in Lyn Macdonald, *1915: The Death of Innocence* (London, 1995). Samples of German Christmas gifts in 1914 are in the IFF collections.

Gerald Burgoyne's diary extract is from *The Burgoyne Diaries* (London, 1985). Captain J. L. Jack's trench diary, ed. John Terraine, appeared as *General Jack's Diary, 1914–1918*

(London, 1964). Malcolm Kennedy's unpublished memoir is in the IWM. *Vize-Feldwebel* Lange is quoted from Caroline Ellen Cooper's *Behind the Lines: One Woman's War,* ed. Decie Denholm (London, 1982). Graham Williams was interviewed in 1981 for a BBC television documentary on the truce by Brown and Seaton (CT). Bruce Bairnsfather wrote and illustrated *Carry On Sergeant!* (Indianapolis, 1927), based upon his annual war years volumes, *Fragments from France,* these familiar as *The Bystander* trench newspaper series.

'If the Sergeant Steals Your Rum' ('The Old Barbed Wire') is reprinted in full in *The Long Trail* above. Joan Littlewood's Theatre Workshop at Stratford East, London, produced *Oh What a Lovely War!* (London, 1963). Its bawdy version of 'Christmas Day in the Workhouse' is drawn from *The Long Trail.* The play's concept emerged from a radio programme, 'A Long, Long Trail', scripted by Charles Chilton and based upon service songs. 'Snoopy's Christmas' (1967), derived from Charles Shultz's beloved cartoon character, was first sung by The Royal Guardsmen and recorded on several pressings, the first by Laurie Records.

The anonymous Royal Field Artillery officer's letter appeared in *The Times* on 1 January, 1915, along with others under 'Letters from the Front, Christmas Truce'—

the first major break in the story in the British press. A flood of published letters followed.

2. CHRISTMAS EVE

Henry Williamson's alter ego hero Phillip Maddison, a kilted Scot (unlike the real-life Williamson), and a lieutenant commissioned in the field (whereas the author, then a private, would receive his commission in England in April 1915 after a Blighty wound), appears in his novel *A Fox Under My Cloak* (London, 1955). A. J. Philip's experience is reported in J. Q. Henriques, *The War History of the 1st Battalion Queen's Westminster Rifles* (London, 1923). French fraternization is described by Charles Toussaint, *Petites Histoires d'un glorieux regiment* (Montvillieres, 1973), quoted in Leonard V. Smith, *Between Mutiny and Obedience* (Princeton, 1994), where other incidents of fraternization up and down the line, with identification of units, are also cited. Additional accounts of French fraternization appear in Alain Barluet, 'Christmas Fraternising', *L'Histoire,* January, 1988, trans. by Michel Pharand. Chaplain Metzger's 'Snapshots from the Field' was published in the *Kölnische Volkszeitung und Handelsblatt,* 13 January, 1915. The 13th Westphalian Regiment's involvement is recorded in detail in Carl Groos, editor, *Infanterie-Regiment*

231

Herwarth von Bittelfeld (1. Westfälisches) Nr. 15 im Weltkriege, 1914–18 (Oldenburg, 1927). James Krüss's *'Der Weilmachtsbaum im Niemandsland'* was first published in *Helfende Hände* (Münster, 1972), issued by the Westphalian Protestant Church, then collected into *Mein Urgrossvater, die Helden, und ich* (Ravensburg, 1972), with illustrations by Rolf Rettich. Heinz Kosok called my attention to the original of this tale. The delightful English translation, *My Great-Grandfather, the Heroes, and I* (New York, 1973, originally published 1967), is by Edelgard von Heydenkampf Brühl. Krüss wrote to SW about the origins of the story on 20 May, 1993.

For the Garhwals see Brig. Gen. J. Evatt, *Historical Record of the 39th Royal Garhwal Rifles, I,* 1887–1922 (Aldershot, n.d.); for letters written by Indian troops in the field see David Omissi, ed., *Indian Voices of the Great War. Soldiers' Letters, 1914–1918* (Oxford, 1999). Some details of the German pump incident are also derived from Gordon Corrigan, *Sepoys in the Trenches* (Staplehurst, 1999).

Berlin Opera tenor Walter Kirchhoff is recalled by French, German and English listeners as well as by Crown Prince Wilhelm in his *My War Experiences* (New York 1923). Walther Stennes is described by Charles Drage in *The Amiable Prussian* (London, 1958). Private Schlump is the anti-hero of the anonymously published novel *Schlump*, trans. Maurice Samuel (London, 1929). Its unidentified author, Emil Schulz, was sixteen in 1914. Carl Muhlegg recalls his experience in *Zeg mij waar de bloemen zijn: Beelden uit de Eerste Werelddoorlog in Vlaandereren (Tell Me Where the Flowers Are: Images from the First World War in Flanders)*, trans. Roland Fleischer and Roelina Berst (Leuven, 1995), IFF. *'Die Feldpostbriefe des Gefreiten Knetschke'*, published as if by an authentic Private Knetschke, appeared in the last issue dated 1914 of *Der Brummer (The Grumbler)*. The translation is by Beate Engel-Doyle. (Knetschke's garbled proverb was identified for me by Ian Halls.)

Malcolm Kennedy's unpublished memoir is in the IWM. Accounts from Scottish units from their letters in contemporary newspapers are numerous. The Cameronians are recorded by Col. H. H. Story in *History of the Cameronians (Scottish Rifles) 1910–1933* (Edinburgh, 1961). For Sir Edward Hulse of the 2nd Scots Guards, see his privately printed letters (1918, posthumous) and *War Letters of Fallen Englishmen,* ed. Laurence Housman (London, 1930). For the German Major Thomas's view of the same scene, with Hulse, see the 25 December, 1934 issue of *D.A.Z.*, a German services publication. A copy is in the IWM's Hulse file. That the Germans sang 'Tipperary' across the line in German is reported, with the words, in the *Belfast Evening Telegraph*, 1 January, 1915. Volume 1 of the war diary of the 14th Brigade, by F. S. Maude, is WO 95/1561 34851 in the Public Record Office. Gaston Durnez quotes the Deseyne brothers on fraternization. See Aleks and André Deseyne, *Zonnebecke, 1914–1918: Death and Resurrection of a Village* (Zonnebecke, 1976), translated from the Dutch by Roelina Berst.

The correspondent impressed with Granier's striking tenor voice wrote in the English monthly *The Lady* in its January, 1915 issue. Victor Granier of the Paris Opera was further identified for me by the staff of the Opera Bastille. Corporal Frobenius and Major Spatling appear in the account by Rupert Frey in *Four Years at the Western Front: History of the Regiment List, 16th R.J.R.*, ed. Fridolin Solleder (Munich, 1952), trans. Gerhard Strasser. Robert de Wilde's memoir is *Mon Journal de Campagne* (Paris, 1918); Karel Lauwers's diary is at IFF, as are his drawings, now strikingly reproduced in *Karel Lauwers, kunstenaar & soldat,* ed. Piet Chielens, Dominiek Dendooven, Jan Dewilde and Annick Vandenbilcke (Ypres, 2000). The Diksmuide monstrance recovery is described in more detail than here by Julian Start and Josef van Ryckeghem in papers now in IFF and in Muhlegg, above.

Hugo Klemm, Johannes Niemann and

Albert Moren are quoted in CT. Charles Brewer's letter to his father was published in the *Bristol Times,* 2 January, 1915; he is also quoted, as is Josef Sewald, in Leslie Baily, *Scrapbook, 1900–1914* (London, 1957). For the complete lyrics of 'Fred Karno's Army', see *The Long Trail,* above. For Percy H. Jones see also above. For the *Bierhalle* version of *'Heil Dir im Siegerkranz'* I am indebted to Jürgen Kamm, who also furnished the original text from the *Deutsches Volksliedarchiv der Universität Freiburg im Bereisgau.* Kurt Zehmisch's diary is from the IFF courtesy of his son, Rudolf Zehmisch, and Dominiek Dendooven, and trans. by Beate Engel-Doyle. Unsigned extracts first appeared in the *Plauener Sonntags-Anzieger,* 15 January, 1915. The substantial involvement of the London Rifles is described in A. S. Bates, C. Harrison Jones, H. G. Wilkinson, et al, *The History of the London Rifle Brigade, 1859–1919* (London, 1921). The shouted 'Where are your Christmas trees?' is from O. F. Bailey and H. M. Hollier, *'The Kensingtons': 13th London Regiment* (London, 1936). 'Rudolf's' letter appeared in *Vorwärts,* 5 January, 1915. W. R. M. Percy's reminiscence is the Christmas 1914 chapter of *The Prudential Staff and the Great War* (London, 1938), compiled by H. F. Boisseau. For Valentine Williams, see above.

3. THE DEAD

For Maddison, see Henry Williamson, above. For Franco-German fraternization see earlier references, Grenadier Thimian's German perspective in CT, and an anonymous letter under the title *'Dokumente der Menschlichkeit'* in the *Frankfurter Zeitung on* 6 January, 1915. Harold de Buriatti's experience is reported in the typescript war diary of the 2nd Battalion of the Bedfordshires Regiment, IWM. For Hugo Klemm and for Percy Jones, see above. R. J. Armes's letter, often reprinted but seldom in full, first appeared in part in *The Times* on 2 January, 1915, without his name, under 'Letters from the Front. More Tales of the Truce'. At this point newspapers across Britain began scrambling for similar accounts from families, offering to pay 'space rates'. Armes's letters were privately (and posthumously) published in 1918, and the key letter to his mother, 28 December, 1914, was reprinted in *War Letters of Fallen Englishmen*, edited by Laurence Housman (London, 1930). A complete reprint is in *Antiquarian Book Monthly Review*, December 1991. In it, also, are many references to Captain George Paynter, referred to here and in later chapters. Stephen Graham's experiences can be found in his *The Challenge of the Dead* (London, 1981). Esslemont Adams (a captain and chaplain) is both quoted and reported in the

London *Daily Mail,* 1 January, 1915 and the *Aberdeen Daily Journal*, 4 January, 1915.

Giles Loder's account is in the Public Record Office as WO 95/1657. For Sewald and Brewer, see above. The football imagery in the rabbit chase is from 'One Day of Peace at the Front', *Daily Mail,* 1 January, 1915. Arthur Pelham-Burn's letter to Cecil Mathew about the burial episode is in the IWM. Alexander Runcie's unpublished memoir is in the IWM. Lothian Nicholson's East Lancashires diary is in the IWM. The letter from a French soldier about Germans and French shouting 'down with the war' slogans is quoted in a dispatch from Paris in the *Manchester Guardian,* 14 January, 1915. The cartoon picturing *poilu* clambering upon a huge Christmas gift pipe, with its French caption, was claimed by the Germans to have been secured on 22 April, 1915, from the possessions of a dead soldier. It was printed by the XXVI Reserve Corps in a collection, *Skizzen aus den Französischen stellungen un Ypern.* A copy is at IFF. Emile Barraud's description is in Alan Barluet; see above. Victor Chapman's letters appear in a memorial volume edited by his father, critic John Jay Chapman, *Victor Chapman's Letters from France* (New York, 1917*)*.

Williamson's reference to Hitler as one of his 'opposite numbers' is in HW's *Goodbye West Country* (London, 1937; Boston, 1938*)*. Many biographies refer to Hitler in 1914 but not always with accuracy. Ian Kershaw's *Hitler,* *1889–1936: Hubris* (New York, 1999) seems the most authoritative recent life. I have also used Charles Bracelen Flood's *Hitler: The Path to Power* (Boston, 1989). Walter Flex's *Das Weihnachtsmärchen des Fünfzigsten Regiments* (Munich, 1940) dated, although then unpublished, from 1914; his *Wanderer zwischen beiden Welten* was published posthumously in 1917. Gustav Riebensaham's papers are in the *Militärarchiv,* Freiburg; his semi-official account is *Infanterie-Regiment Prinz Friedrich der Niederlande (2. Westfälisches) Nr. 15 Im Weltkrieg, 1914–18* (Minden, 1931).

4. OUR FRIENDS, THE ENEMY

W. J. Quinton's memoir is in the IWM and quoted from in CT. For Armes, see above. John Ferguson's account (in which he identified himself only as 'Fergie') is 'Christmas in the Trenches', *The Saturday Review* (London), 25 December, 1915. For Bairnsfather, see above. Bryan Latham's reminiscence is *A Territorial Soldier's War* (Aldershot, 1967). For Zehmisch, see above. The German gifts of barrels of beer (exchanged for Tickler's jam) are reported by Private Lyall in a letter to his wife, published in the *Manchester Guardian,* 15 January, 1915, and in Frank Richards's memoir *Old Soldiers*

Never Die (London, 1933). His commanding officer, Captain Stockwell, is quoted at length in J. C. Dunn, *The War the Infantry Knew, 1914–1918* (London, 1938; rept. London, 1987), a chronicle of the Royal Welch Fusiliers. (A letter by Private Frank Devine of the 6th Gordons, Edinburgh *Scotsman,* 2 January, 1915, describes the German poster equivalents.)

For the full lyrics of 'Plum and Apple' and 'M and V' see *The Long Trail,* above. Charles Smith is quoted from his *War History of the 6th Battalion/The Cheshire Regiment* (London, 1932) as compiled from the battalion's war diaries. For the *Pickelhaube* saga, see the history of the London Rifles, above. Graham Williams's unpublished *Saturday Afternoon Soldiers* is quoted in CT. The barter of an issue of *Punch* is described from personal experience in the diary of Lieutenant V. S. F. Hawkins of the Lancashires, IWM, and in his letter in the *Daily Telegraph.* The letter is Owen Seaman's source for his *Punch* satire of the event. Capt. C. A. E. Chudleigh's unpublished memoir is in the IWM. For the Garhwals and their English officers, see above, and also General Drake-Brockman's *With the Royal Garhwal Rifles in the Great War from August 1914 to November 1917* (London, 1934). For William Douglas Home's play, *Christmas Truce*, see details next chapter, where it has more importance. The story of 'Harry' and the

German lieutenant appears in *Trench Yarns for Subalterns and Others* (London, n.d.), by 'Peter', and would be highly suspect if not attributed to the extraordinary conditions at Christmas 1914, where the impossible became the reality. John Reith's remarkable Christmas dinner is described in his memoirs, *Into the Wind* (London, 1949) and *Wearing Spurs* (London, 1966).

The German press carried extensive details of the Kaiser's Christmas at Spa. The text of the Kaiser's Christmas harangue to his officers is in J. E. Edmonds and G. C. Wynne, *Military Operations, France and Belgium, 1915* (London, 1927). Edmonds and Wynne also furnish an account of Douglas Haig's Christmas.

For further French fraternizing, see earlier references, continued here. The French captain's elaborate concert for the enemy is described by J. Maxtone Graham in *Kiwanis Magazine,* December 1964/January 1965. Brigadier Gleichen's view about command toleration of fraternizing is in his *The Doings of the Fifteenth Infantry Brigade. August 1914 to March 1915* (Edinburgh and London, 1917).

The wry 'Living it Up' song, text by Lester Simpson, is recorded from performances in December 1998 of *'Kerrstbestand—Christmas Truce',* by the group Wak Maar Proper in Ieper Cathedral and in Diksmuide, as *Christmas 1914* on No Masters disc NMCD 14 (1999).

5. FOOTBALL

For Captain J. L. Jack's wartime trench diary, see above. Maddison's semifictional adventures are continued from Williamson's *A Fox under My Cloak*. 'The Greater Game' football cartoon appeared in *Punch* on 21 October, 1914. The football-minded British recruiting poster is described in George L. Mosse, *Fallen Soldiers: Reshaping the Memory of the World Wars* (New York, 1990). The *Glasgow News,* 2 January, 1915, reported in a letter from 'an officer' that a Saxon claimed to have toured in 1913 with a Leipzig team that beat Glasgow Celtic 1-0, but according to E. Christian, 'The Christmas Truce', *Gun Fire: A Journal of First World War History* (28, 1994), the records do not support the boast. A similar account appeared in the London *Morning Post,* 2 January, 1915. A photocopy of H. Barrington-Brown's handwritten three-page memoir, 'Christmas Truce 1914' is in IFF.

Private Tapp is quoted in CT. The official denial, despite testimony from participants, that a Rifles Brigade match occurred with the Germans, is in A. S. Bates, C. Harrison Jones, H. G. Wilkinson et al., *The History of the London Rifle Brigade, 1859–1919* (London, 1921). The account by the Wray brothers, who also published 'Christmas 1914' in *The Army Quarterly*, October 1968, is from a three-page transcript (photocopy) in the IFF. W. V.

Mathews was quoted earlier from the chronicle of the Rifle Brigade, but that account was preceded by his testimony in the London *Evening News*, 2 January, 1915. G. A. Farmer's account, 'Quite As Peaceful As You in Good Old England', appeared in the *Leicestershire Mail,* 6 January, 1915. Albert Winn's reminiscence appears in *Poor Bloody Murder: Personal Memoirs of the First World War*, ed. Gordon Reid (Calgary, 1980). The French recollection of the kilted Scot footballers is in *'Il y a 60 ans sur le front: La Leçon de Noel'*, in an unidentified newspaper clipping recalling the event dated 24 December, 1974 (IFF).

Johannes Niemann's letters, about what some Scot footballers wore under their kilts, and about what Hugo Klemm remembered, trans. by Gerhard Strasser, are from IFF. The football account from the *Das. 9 Köninglich Säschsische Infanterie-Regiment Nr. 133 Im Weltkrieg 1914–18* (IWM) is translated by SW. A. (Bob) Lovell's letter first appeared in the *London Evening News*, 2 January, 1915; he emerges again in *The Rifle Brigade Chronicle 1914.* For Zehmisch and Brewer see above. Fred Langton's letter was in the *Yorkshire Post,* 7 January, 1915. Corporal Hunt's letter appeared in the *Sheffield Daily Telegraph*, 4 January, 1915. Lieutenant Richards's letter appeared in the *Manchester Guardian* on 12 January, 1915. The unnamed infantry

242

colonel's New Year's challenge to the Germans is described by him in a letter to his wife published in the *Daily Telegraph* on 2 January, 1915. For Alexander Runcie, see above. Private Gilbert of the Kensingtons is quoted from a letter in IWM. Ernie Williams is quoted from CT. Sergeant-Major F. Nadin's account is in the *Cheshire Observer*, 9 January, 1915. Captain Thomas Laurence Frost's letter of 31 December, 1914, to his father was copied for me by his great-nephew, John Furlong, on 17 November, 2000. Frost was with the 1st Battalion, 22nd Cheshire Regiment, 15th Infantry Brigade. He was killed on 28 March, 1915, and is buried at Zillebeke, near Ypres. Robert Graves's well-researched short story, 'Christmas Truce', is collected in his *Complete Short Stories*, ed. Lucia Graves (New York, 1995). It first appeared as 'Wave No Banners' in *The Saturday Evening Post*, 15 December, 1962. He did not join the Welch Fusiliers on the line until early 1915. The Blackadder dialogue is from *Blackadder Goes Forth: The Historic Fourth Series* (BBCV 4787, tape 2), a blackly satiric sitcom written by Ben Elton and Richard Curtis and first shown in 1989 (Richard Atkins collection, London). Coincidentally, a T. Blackadder of the Royal Irish Rifles, who died in battle on 24 March, 1917, is buried at the Pond Farm Cemetery at Wulvergem, near Ypres. The Commonwealth

War Graves Commission records five other Blackadders, four of whom were with units on the line at Christmas 1914.

William Douglas Home's play *A Christmas Truce* (London, 1990) was first performed at the Haymarket, Basingstoke, 9 November, 1989.

Guardsman Harold Bryan's letter to his family is quoted by Geoffrey Parkhouse in 'The Miracle of No Man's Land', *The Sunday Express*, 22 December, 1974. Private Goggin's remarkable letter about a bayonet fight to the death, which strains belief, appeared in the *Manchester Guardian* on 14 January, 1915.

The letter from the 5th Scottish Rifles sergeant from Longside is in the *Glasgow News*, 2 January, 1915. The 'Grand Ducal Sovereign' comment is in a letter by an unnamed subaltern in the *Liverpool Daily Post and Mercury*, 6 January, 1915. William Dawkins is quoted in *Zeg mij waar de bloemen zijn* (see above). C. E. M. Richards's memoir is in IWM. Private Mullard's letter is from the *Daily Telegraph*, 2 January, 1915. For Riebensahn, see above. Emphasizing the centrality of football in the British mythos of the truce is Michael Foreman's illustrated novella about football in No Man's Land at Christmas 1914, *War Game* (London, 1989, rept. 1995), intended for young readers. The Football Association Premier League Hall of Fame exhibited briefly in the former County

Hall, Riverside Building, Westminster Bridge Road, London.

6. HOW IT ENDED

The syndicated 'Hop' cartoon appeared in American newspapers on 26 December, 1914. Ernst Jünger's autobiographical novel *In Stahlgewittern* (1920), translated as *Storm of Steel,* is subtitled *'Aus dem Tagebuch* [diary] *eines Stosstruppführers'.* The Guards officer on enemy friendliness is quoted by Tony Ashworth in *Trench Warfare, 1914–1918: The Live and Let Live System* (New York, 1980). A photocopy of H. Barrington-Brown's handwritten three-page memoir, 'Christmas Truce 1914', is in IFF. For Hulse, see above. The German barbers who had worked in England and were encountered on the other side of the line during the truce is one of the subjects of Captain D. Mackenzie's *The Sixth Gordons in France and Flanders* (Aberdeen, 1921) as well as a phenomenon written about by Graham. For Graham Williams, see above. The German juggler (not a figment of Graves's fictionalization) is characterized as a potential Pied Piper by Reginald Berkeley in *The History of the Rifle Brigade in the War of 1914–1918, I* (London, 1927). For Robert Graves and Bob Lovell, see above. Major Jeffreys is quoted in J. M. Craster, ed., *Fifteen*

Rounds a Minute: The Grenadiers at War, 1914 (London, 1976). Captain Congreve's *Armageddon Road: A VC's Diary* (London, 1982) was edited by Terry Norman. Sergeant W. Jones's letter appeared in the *South Wales Weekly Argus,* 16 January, 1915. Alfred Dougan Chater's Christmas Day letter to his mother is in IWM. John Erskine's letter appeared in the *Edinburgh Evening News,* 12 January, 1915. For J. L. Jack, see above. *The Landwehr* lieutenant's letter was published, unsigned, by *The Times* on 28 January, 1915.

The French *fléchette* aerial dart was illustrated in the *Daily Telegraph* on 2 January, 1915. Letters by Major Archibald Buchanan-Dunlop are quoted in CT; the first story in the press about him appeared in the London *Daily Sketch* on 5 January, 1915. General Congreve is quoted in his son's diary. For Paynter and Hulse, see above. For Perry Jones, see his diary, in IWM. Rifleman Eade's letter appeared in the London *Evening News,* 2 January, 1915. For Tapp, see above. The chaplaincy satire ('It is a Christian virtue/To lay you in the dust') is quoted in J. G. Fuller, *Troop Morale and Popular Culture in the British and Dominion Armies, 1914–1918* (Oxford, 1990). For Armes, see above.

Herbert Sulzbach is quoted from his *With the German Guns: Four Years on the Western Front,* 1914–1918 (rept. Hamden, CT, 1981), trans. Richard Thonger from *Zwei lebende*

Mauern. For William Williamson, see his diary, as quoted in CT. The French attacks on Steinbach are from Martin Gilbert (above) and French official reports of the failed war in Alsace. Captain F. D. Harris wrote to his family in a letter published by the *Liverpool Daily Post & Mercury,* 4 January, 1915. For Captain Stockwell, see above. For Victor Chapman's letters, see above. The German deserter's army war memoir, translated by J. Koettgen, is *A German Deserter's Experience* (New York, 1917). For Frank Richards and Corporal Ferguson, see above. For Smith-Dorrien, see above. Drummond is quoted in CT. Wenzl, Bossert and Meinecke appear in Rupert Frey's *'Becoming Brothers between the Fronts'. Four Years at the Western Front. The History of the Regiment List. 16th R.J.R.,* edited by Fridolin Solleder, trans. Beate Engel-Doyle (Munich, 1952).

For William Tapp, see above. Vera Brittain is quoted from her memoir *Testament of Youth* (London, 1933). Lieutenant Bolz's diary (IFF) is quoted in *The 8th Württemberg Infantry Regiment No. 126 Grand Duke Frederick of Baden During the World War of 1914–1918,* ed. Major General D. Glück and Major General D. Wald (Stuttgart, 1929). Wedderburn-Maxwell's letters are in the IWM. Churchill's 'chew barbed wire' image is described in a letter from Prime Minister H. H. Asquith to Venetia Stanley, Martin Gilbert, ed., *Winston*

S. Churchill: Companion Volume III, Part I, July 1914–April 1915 (New York, 1973). The Alsatians quoted are in *The 5th Lower Alsatian Infantry Regiment No. 143 in Peace and in World War,* by Captain Hans Bossert (Berlin, 1935), trans. Beate Engel-Doyle.

Major Dickins's New Year's Eve account is from Cuthbert Keeson, *History and Records of Queen Victoria's Rifles* (London, 1923). For the fictional Private Schlump, and for Smith and Thomas, see above.

The apocryphal story of the grisly ambush of German fraternizers is by Alexander Woollcott: 'By Word of Mouth', *American Legion Magazine,* July 1931. Hubert Griffith's play, *Tunnel Trench,* was published in London in 1924. For Bairnsfather, see above. While the cease-fire flickered out in many sectors, there are also accounts of respectful and dignified endings of the truce, as with the 6th Division's ceremonial ending, described by a British officer in Tony Ashworth, *Trench Warfare, 1914–1918: The Live and Let Live System* (New York, 1980).

7. WHAT IF—?

Reclams Universum (Leipzig, 1915) published two dispatches as well as three artists' depictions from London papers—the *Sphere,* the *Graphic,* and the *Illustrated London News,* ostensibly to disprove them. When German wartime censorship was lifted, the evidence of servicemen's cameras disproved the denials.

The invasion strategies are described in detail in John Keegan's *The First World War* (London, 1998). Although the plans were updated over a twenty-year period, the quick victory envisaged failed to happen. *Bernard Shaw's Letters to Siegfried Trebitsch* (Stanford, 1986) are edited by Samuel A. Weiss. For Captain Jack, see above. The German map of a post-victory Europe appeared in Frederick James Gregg, 'The Map of Europe, in 1915', *Vanity Fair*, January 1915. Lyn Macdonald is quoted from *1915: The Death of Innocence*, above. Sir Kingsley Wood's speech in the Commons, 31 March, 1930, appears in full in *Parliamentary Debates: Official Report. Fifth Series, Volume 237* (1930), for the period 24 March through 17 April, 1930. Wilfrid Ewart is in *When Armageddon Came: Studies in Peace and War* (London, 1933). Folksinger John McCutcheon's 'Christmas in the Trenches', about an officer named Ian Calhoun, was recorded by Rounder Records, Cambridge, MA, in 1985. What actually happened to Sir Iain Colquhoun is reported by Robert Blake (ed.) in *The Private Papers of Douglas Haig 1914–1919* (London, 1952).

The Farm, the rock band lamenting about 'nothing learned and nothing gained' recorded 'All Together Now', about the Flanders trenches, on an album titled *Spartacus* (BMG CD, 1991). Frederick Niven's 'A Carol from Flanders', dated Christmas 1914, was first published in *The Athenaeum* (London) and *The Living Age* (Boston) in 1915, then in *In Flanders Fields and Other Poems* (New York, n.d.) as well as in *A Lover of the Land and Other Poems* (New York, 1925). Only the closing quatrain is quoted here.

38002010550327

ACKNOWLEDGMENTS

I am indebted to an army of loyal and resourceful scholars, informants, translators and intermediaries, some of whom have worked with me for more than a decade. They include Maartje Abbenhuis, Lucy Addington, Jean-Claude Amalric, Richard Atkins, Roelina Berst, Suzy Brain-England, Patrick Bridgewater, Malcolm Brown, Michael Broyles, Robert Cowley, the late Fred Crawford, Dominiek Dendooven, Delwyn Dennis, Jan DeWilde, M. A. Diefenbach, Robert C. Doyle, Vivian Elliot, Beate Engel-Doyle, Michael England, Roland Fleischer, Colleen Franklin, Robert Freeborn, Dan Freedberg, John Furlong, Paul Fussell, Katrin Hallen, Ian Halls, Alan Hanley-Browne, Eileen Hanley-Browne, M. A. Haug, David Heal, Nicholas Hellen, Christina Holstein, Leon Hugo, Jürgen Kamm, Holger Klein, Heinz Kosok, the late James Krüss, Lannie Liggera, the late Charles W. Mann, George Mauner, Tom Morgan, Bruce Nichols, David Omissi, Michel Pharand, Shirley Rader, Susan Reighard, Simon Robbins, Barbara Ryan, Hedwig Schwall, Alexander Seabrook, Willa Silverman, Markus Spiecker, F. K. Stanzel, Sandra Stelts, Barbara Stelzl-Marx, Gerhard Strasser, Christine Thrower, Tom Vincent,

Sally R. Warren, David A. Weintraub, Rodelle Weintraub, Richard E. Winslow III, Philip Winsor, Peter Zimmerman.

We hope you have enjoyed this Large Print book. Other Chivers Press or Thorndike Press Large Print books are available at your library or directly from the publishers.

For more information about current and forthcoming titles, please call or write, without obligation, to:

Chivers Press Limited
Windsor Bridge Road
Bath BA2 3AX
England
Tel. (01225) 335336

OR

Thorndike Press
295 Kennedy Memorial Drive
Waterville
Maine 04901
USA

All our Large Print titles are designed for easy reading, and all our books are made to last.